POP/ROCK BASS BIBLE

Music transcriptions by Steve Gorenberg

ISBN 0-634-08930-7

7777 W. BLUEMOUND RD. P.O. BOX 13819 MILWAUKEE, WI 53213

For all works contained herein:
Unauthorized copying, arranging, adapting, recording or public performance is an infringement of copyright.
Infringers are liable under the law.

Visit Hal Leonard Online at
www.halleonard.com

TABLE OF CONTENTS

4	ALL I WANNA DO	Sheryl Crow
12	BAD LOVE	Eric Clapton
22	BENNIE AND THE JETS	Elton John
31	BROWN EYED GIRL	Van Morrison
38	CAN'T STAND LOSING YOU	The Police
42	CHEAP SUNGLASSES	ZZ Top
47	CRAZY LITTLE THING CALLED LOVE	Queen
51	DON'T STOP BELIEVIN'	Journey
58	DREAM POLICE	Cheap Trick
66	FASCINATION STREET	The Cure
64	FLY AWAY	Lenny Kravitz
69	GOOD TIMES	Chic
73	HEART AND SOUL	Huey Lewis and the News
80	I DID IT	Dave Matthews Band
89	IT CAN HAPPEN	Yes
99	THE JOKER	Steve Miller Band

109	LADY IN RED	Chris DeBurgh
118	MANEATER	Hall & Oates
128	NO REPLY AT ALL	Genesis
138	ONE THING LEADS TO ANOTHER	The Fixx
144	RIKKI DON'T LOSE THAT NUMBER	Steely Dan
151	R.O.C.K. IN THE U.S.A.	John Cougar Mellencamp
157	SMOOTH OPERATOR	Sade
165	STUCK IN THE MIDDLE WITH YOU	Stealers Wheel
171	SUFFRAGETTE CITY	David Bowie
179	THRILLER	Michael Jackson
187	TURN THE PAGE	Bob Seger & The Silver Bullet Band
195	VERONICA	Elvis Costello
202	WEREWOLVES OF LONDON	Warren Zevon
207	WHEN THE HEART RULES THE MIND	GTR
216	YOU OUGHTA KNOW	Alanis Morissette

224 *Bass Notation Legend*

All I Wanna Do

Words and Music by Kevin Gilbert, David Baerwald, Sheryl Crow, Wyn Cooper and Bill Bottrell

Copyright © 1993 Sony/ATV Tunes LLC, Almo Music Corp., Zen Of Iniquity, Warner-Tamerlane Publishing Corp.,
Old Crow Music, WB Music Corp., Canvas Mattress Music and Ignorant Music
All Rights on behalf of Sony/ATV Tunes LLC Administered by Sony/ATV Music Publishing, 8 Music Square West, Nashville, TN 37203
All Rights on behalf of Zen Of Iniquity Administered by Almo Music Corp.
International Copyright Secured   All Rights Reserved

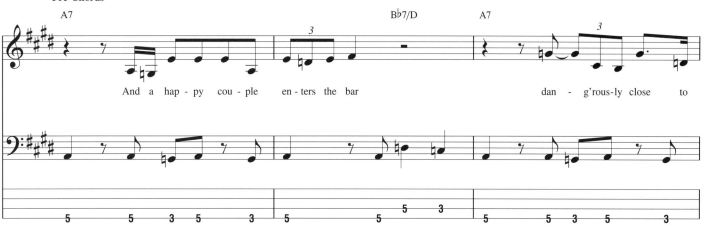
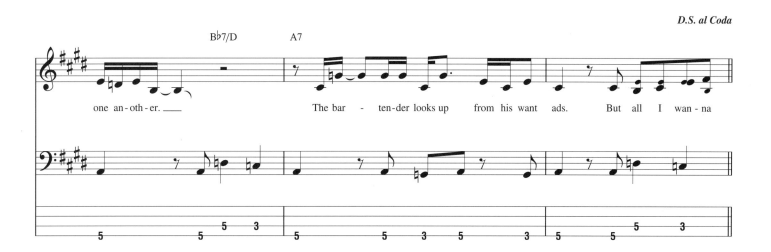
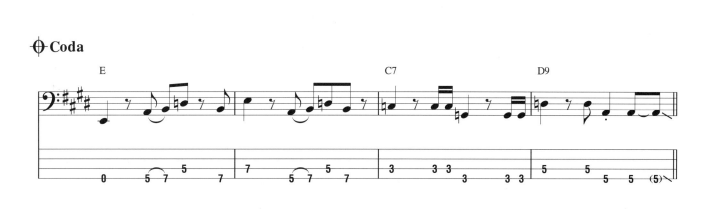

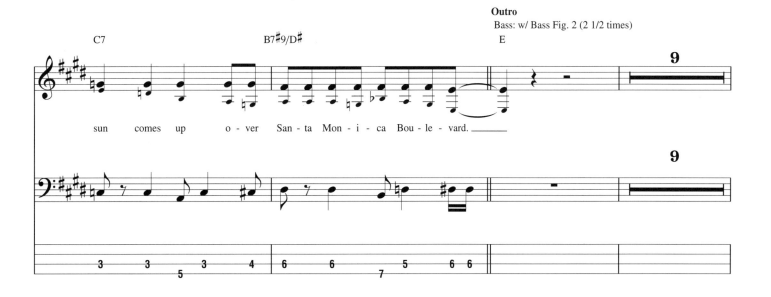
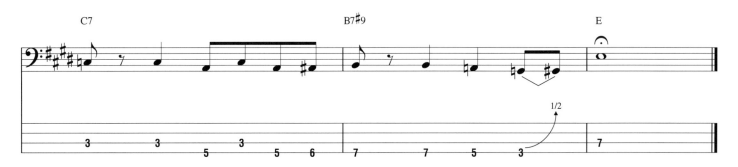

Bad Love

Words and Music by Eric Clapton and Mick Jones

Fretless bass, Drop D tuning:
(low to high) D-A-D-G

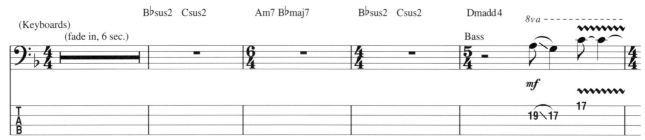

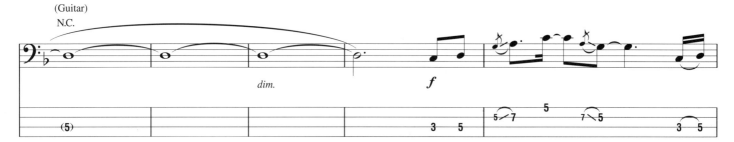

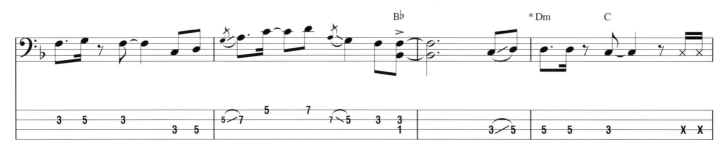

*Chord symbols implied by overall harmony.

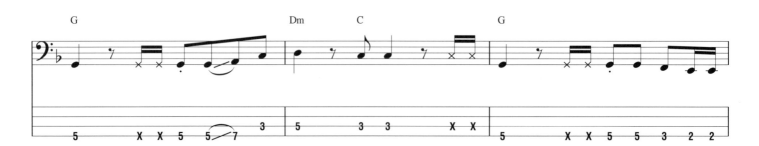

Copyright © 1989 by E.C. Music Ltd. and Heavy Petal Music
All Rights for E.C. Music Ltd. in the U.S. Administered by Unichappell Music Inc.
International Copyright Secured   All Rights Reserved

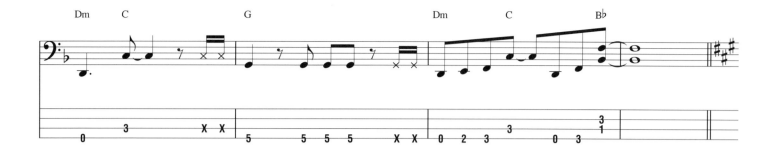

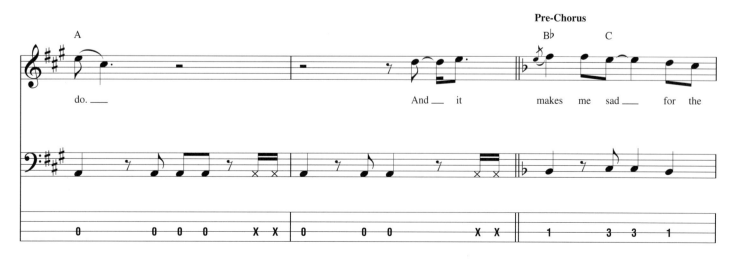

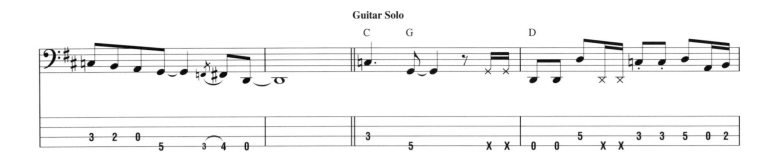
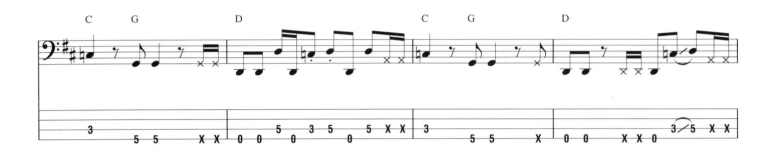
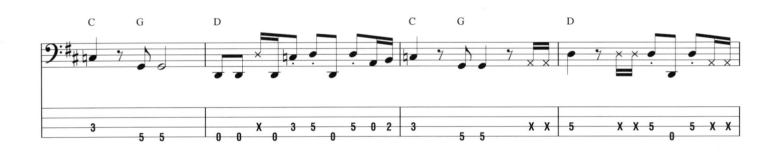

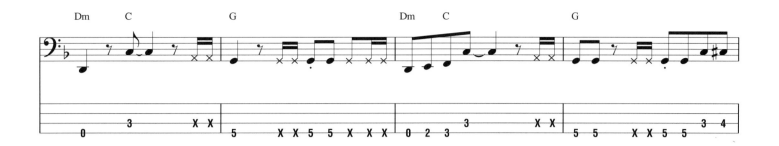

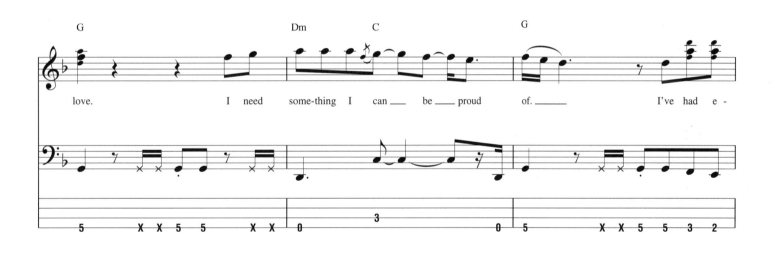
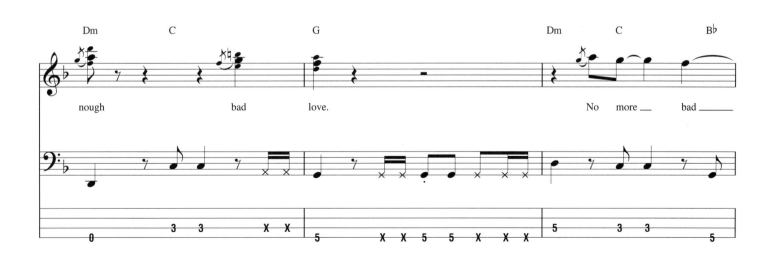

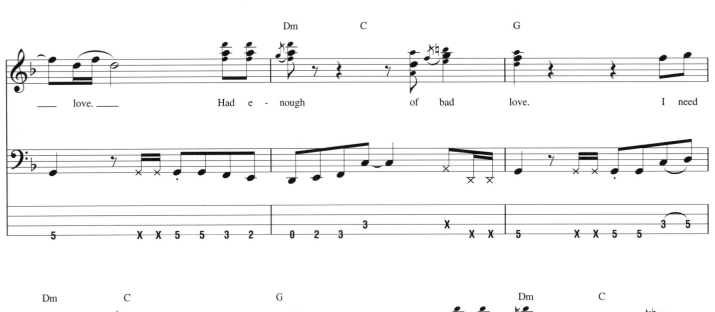

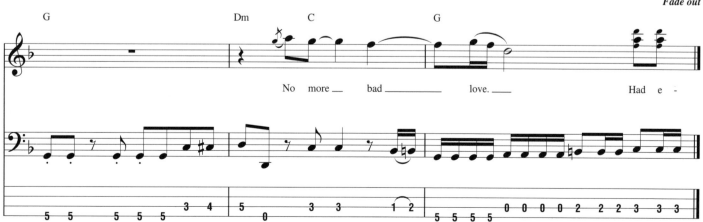

Bennie and the Jets
Words and Music by Elton John and Bernie Taupin

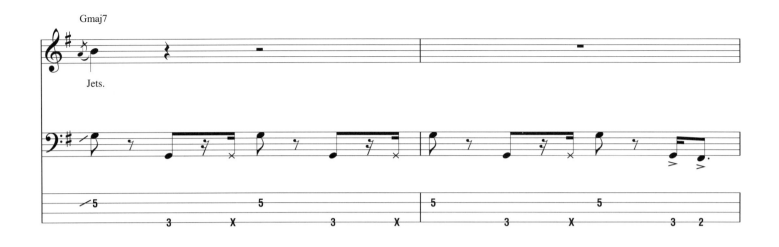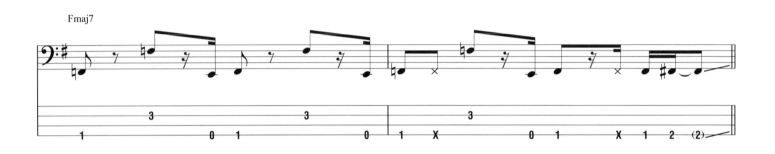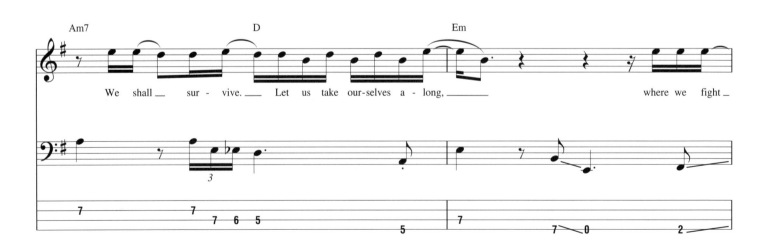

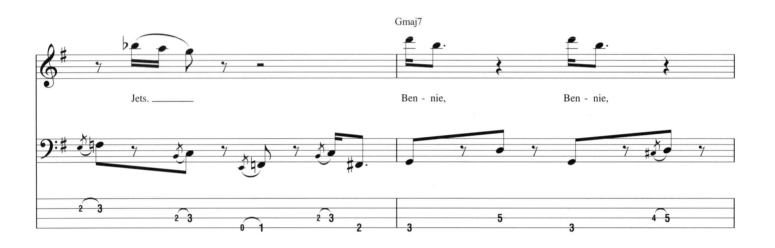

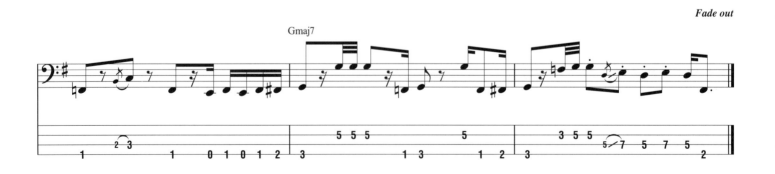

Brown Eyed Girl

Words and Music by Van Morrison

Copyright © 1967 UNIVERSAL MUSIC PUBLISHING INTERNATIONAL LTD.
Copyright Renewed
All Rights for the U.S. and Canada Controlled and Administered by UNIVERSAL - SONGS OF POLYGRAM INTERNATIONAL, INC.
All Rights Reserved   Used by Permission

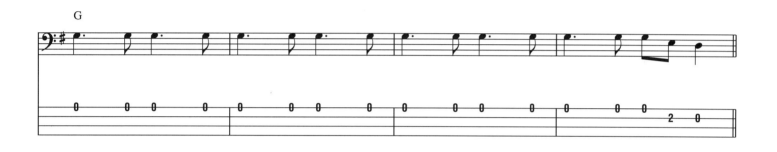
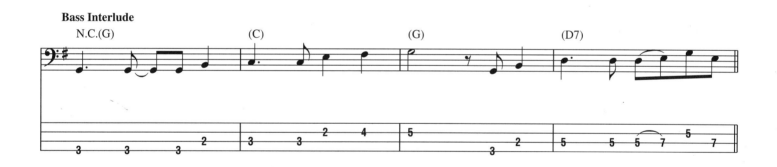

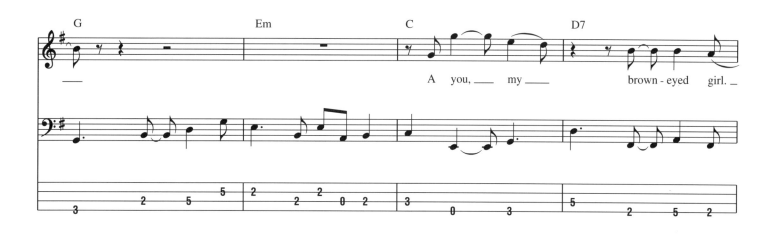

Can't Stand Losing You

Music and Lyrics by Sting

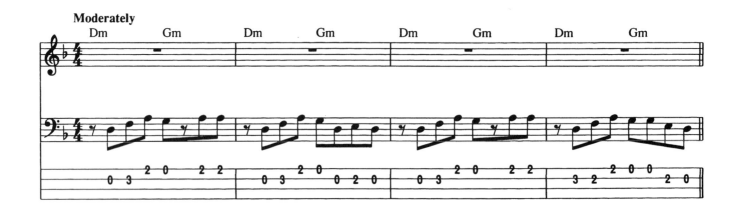

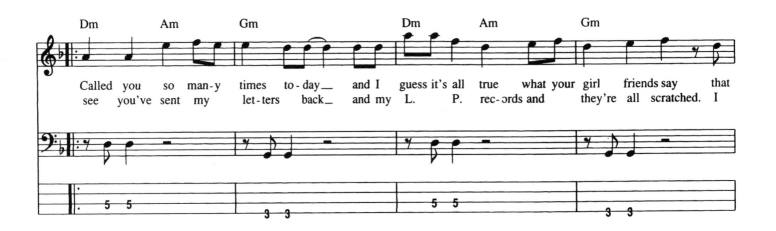

Called you so man-y times to-day and I guess it's all true what your girl friends say that
See you've sent my let-ters back and my L. P. rec-ords and they're all scratched. I

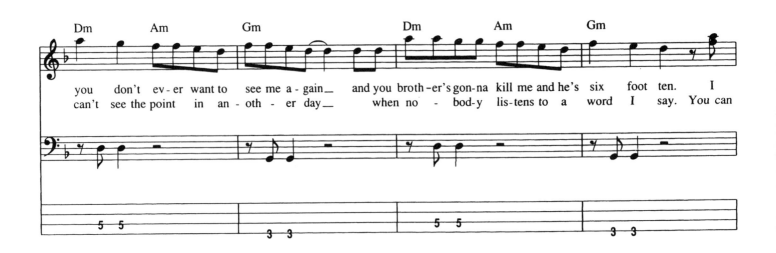

you don't ev-er want to see me a-gain and you broth-er's gon-na kill me and he's six foot ten. I
can't see the point in an-oth-er day when no-bod-y lis-tens to a word I say. You can

© 1978 G.M. SUMNER
Administered by EMI MUSIC PUBLISHING LIMITED
All Rights Reserved   International Copyright Secured   Used by Permission

Cheap Sunglasses

Words and Music by Billy F Gibbons, Dusty Hill and Frank Beard

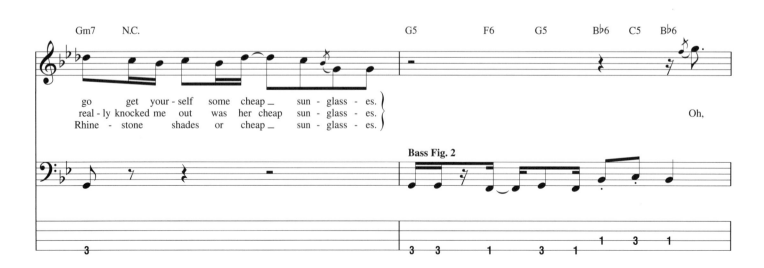

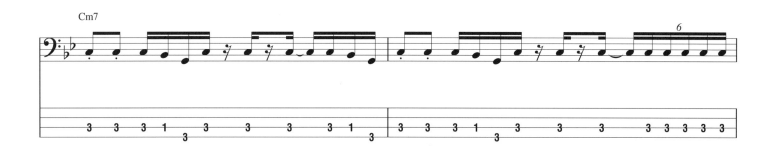

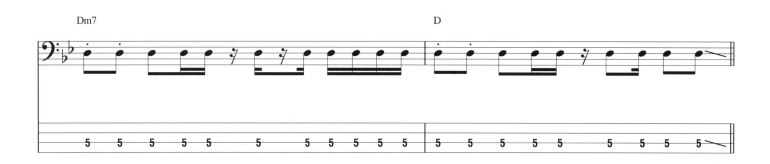

Interlude

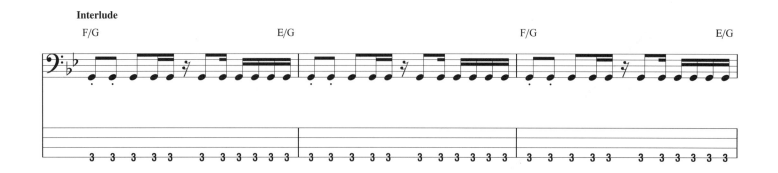

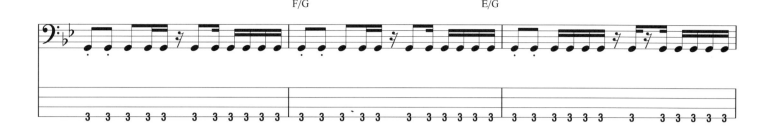
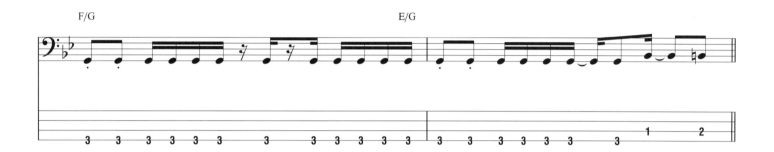
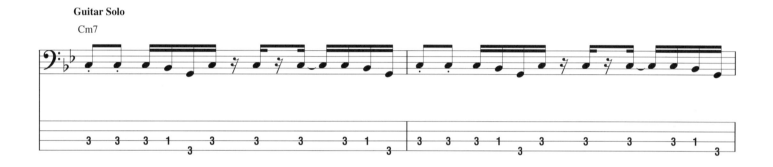
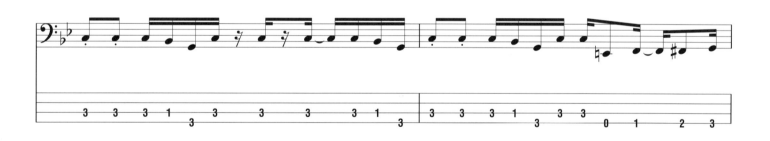
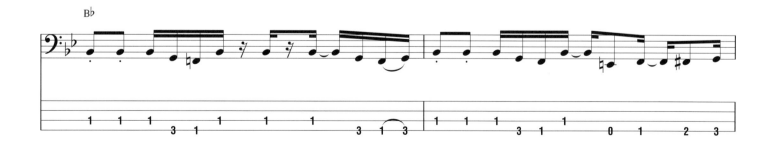

45

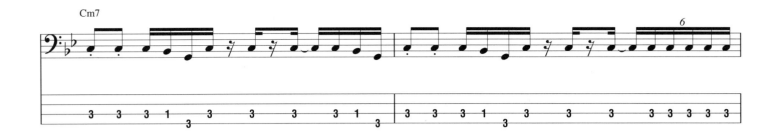

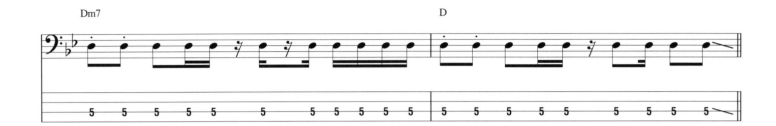

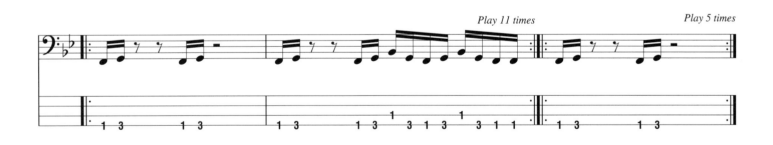

Crazy Little Thing Called Love

Words and Music by Freddie Mercury

© 1979 QUEEN MUSIC LTD.
All Rights for the U.S. and Canada Controlled and Administered by BEECHWOOD MUSIC CORP.
All Rights for the world excluding the U.S. and Canada Controlled and Administered by EMI MUSIC PUBLISHING LTD.
All Rights Reserved   International Copyright Secured   Used by Permission

Don't Stop Believin'

Words and Music by Steve Perry, Neal Schon and Jonathan Cain

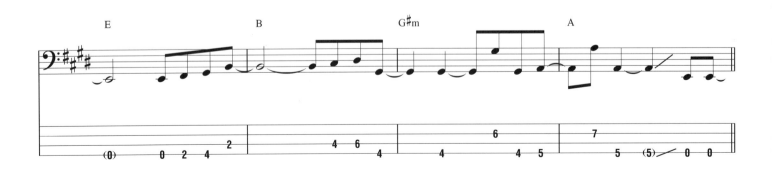

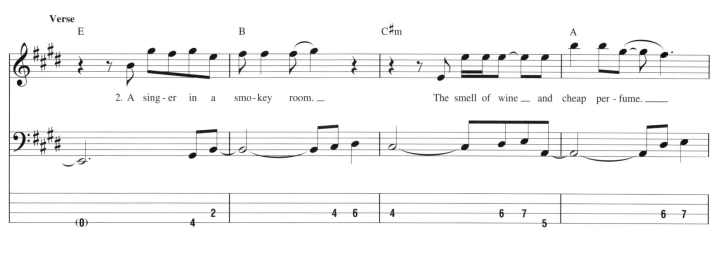
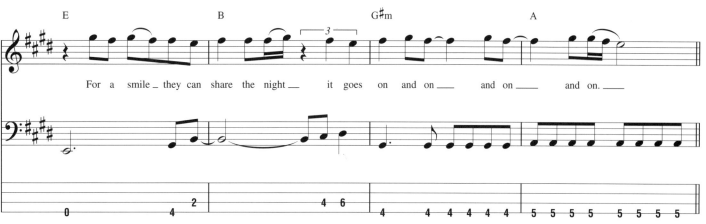

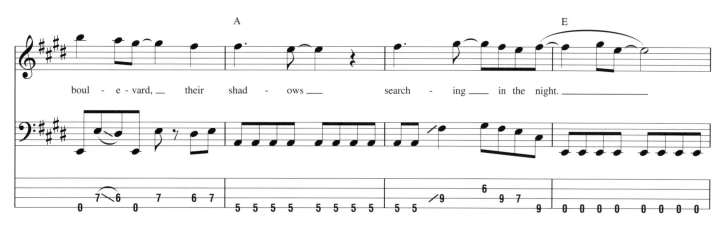

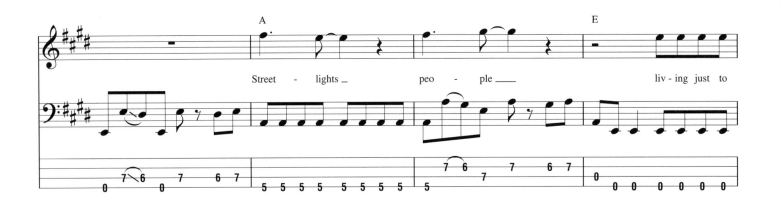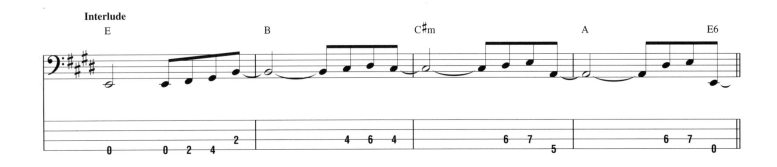

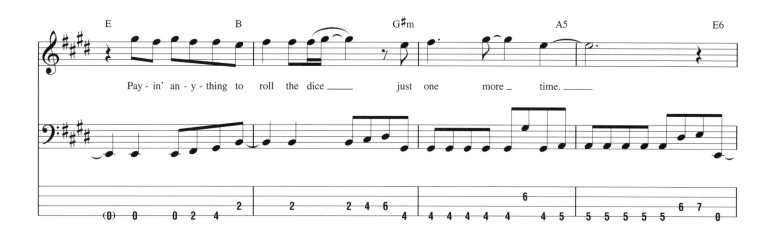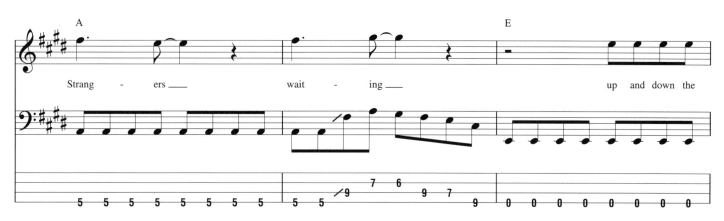

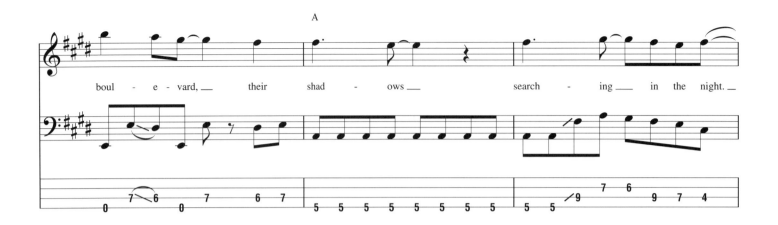
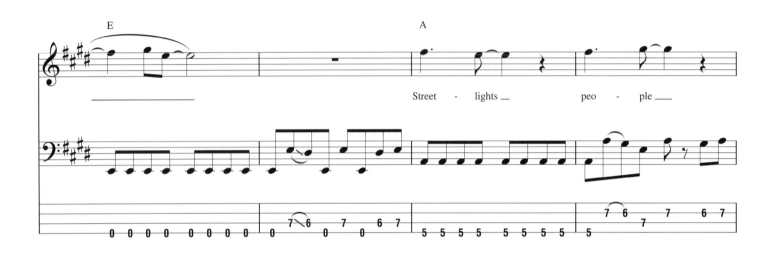
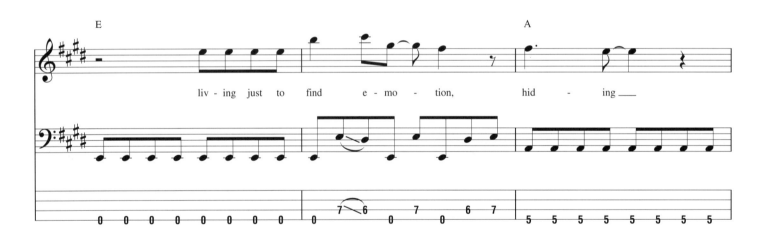
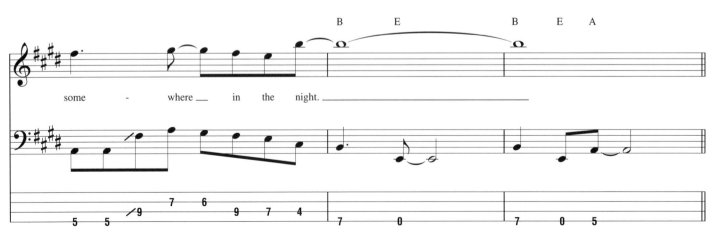

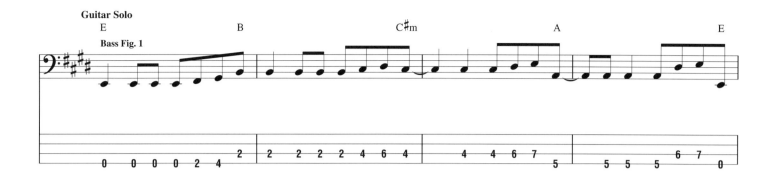
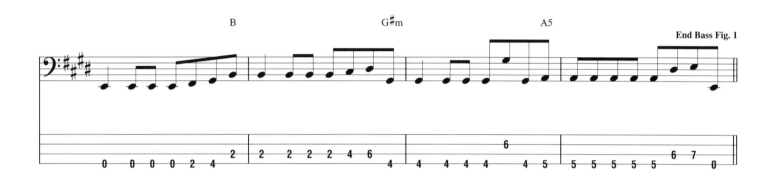

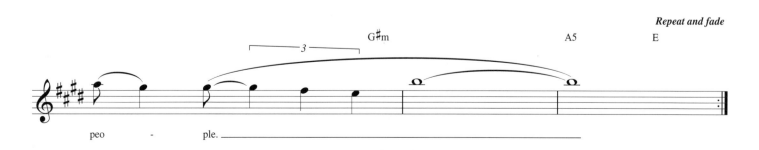

57

Dream Police

Words and Music by Rick Nielsen

5 String bass:
(low to high) B-E-A-D-G

Intro
Moderate Rock ♩ = 136

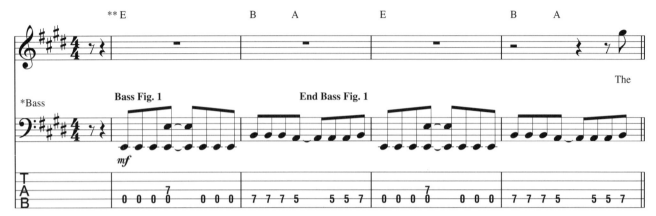

*12 string bass (6 string with each string doubled an octave higher) arranged for 5 string.
**Chord symbols reflect implied tonality.

© 1979 SCREEN GEMS-EMI MUSIC INC. and ADULT MUSIC
All Rights Controlled and Administered by SCREEN GEMS-EMI MUSIC INC.
All Rights Reserved   International Copyright Secured   Used by Permission

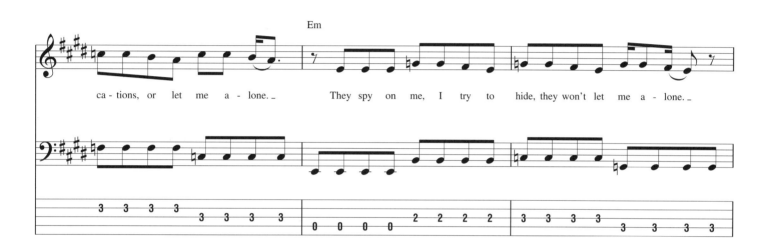
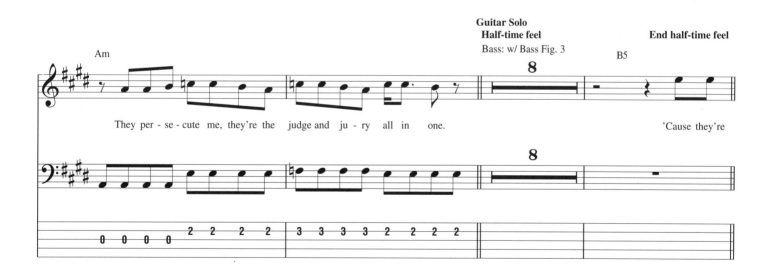

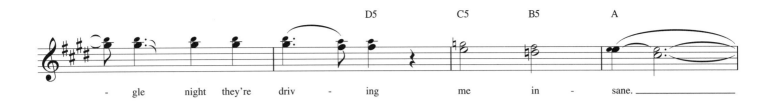
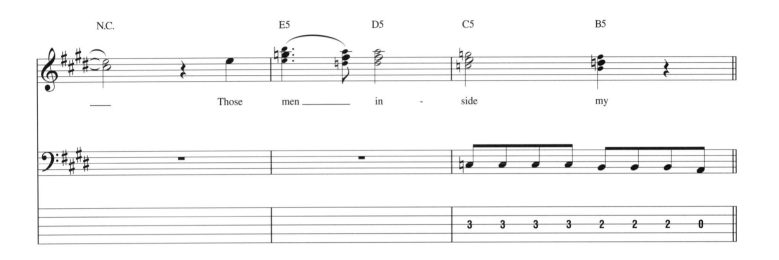
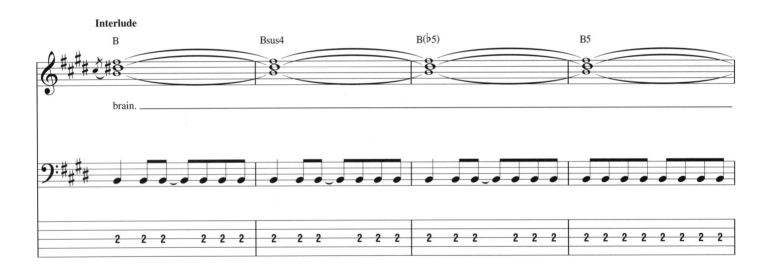
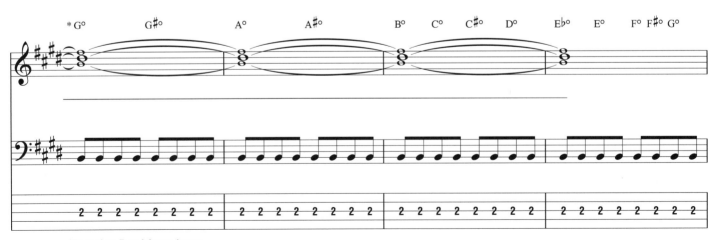

*Bass plays B pedal next 4 meas.

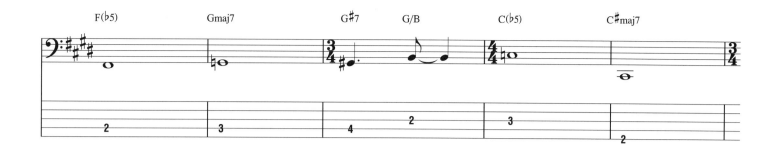
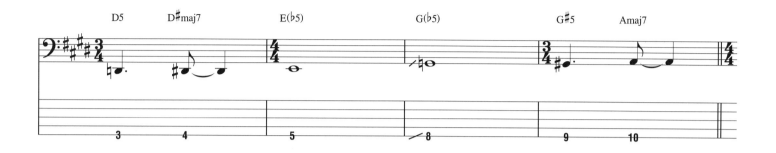
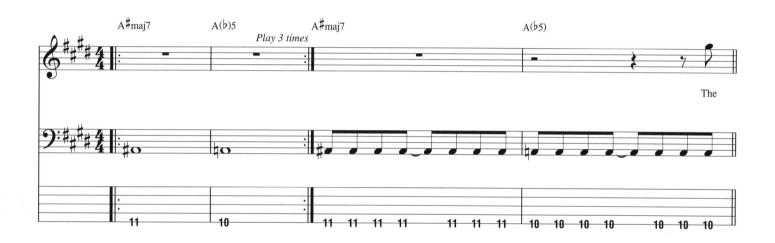

Outro-Chorus
Bass: w/ Bass Fig. 1 (fill fade)

dream po - lice, __ they live in - side of my head. __ The dream po - lice, __ they come to me in my bed. __ The
(Live in - side of my head.) (Come to me in my bed.) __

Play 6 times and fade

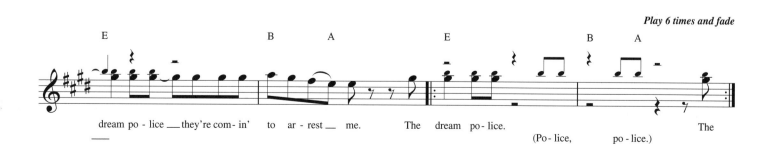

dream po - lice __ they're com - in' to ar - rest me. The dream po - lice. The
(Po - lice, po - lice.)

63

Fascination Street

Words and Music by Robert Smith, Laurence Tolhurst, Simon Gallup, Paul Thompson, Boris Williams and Roger O'Donnell

Tune down 1/2 step:
(low to high) E♭-A♭-D♭-G♭

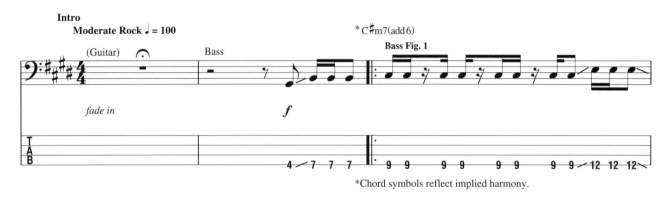

*Chord symbols reflect implied harmony.

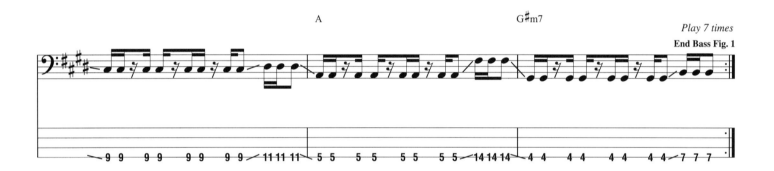

Oh, it's o-pen-ing time down on

Fas-ci-na-tion Street, so let's cut the con-ver-sa-tion and get out for a bit. 'Cause I

Copyright © 1989 by Fiction Songs Ltd.
All Rights for the world Administered by BMG Music Publishing Ltd.
All Rights for the U.S. Administered by BMG Songs, a division of BMG Music Publishing NA, Inc.
International Copyright Secured   All Rights Reserved

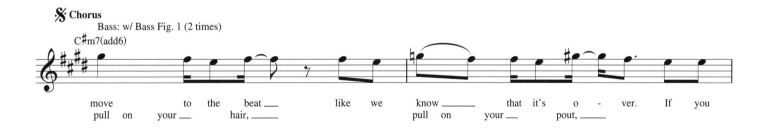
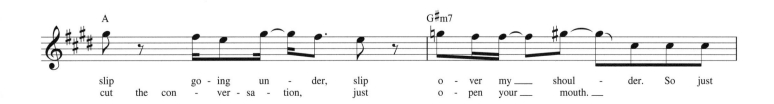

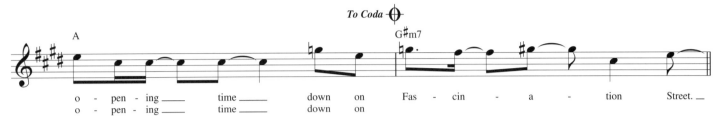
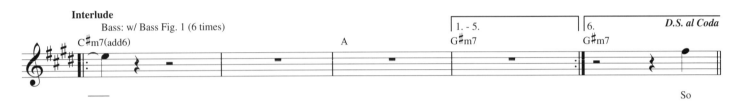

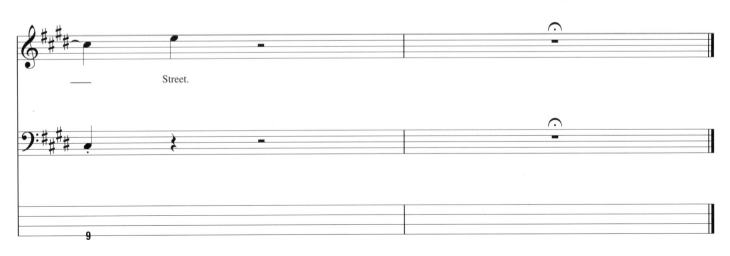

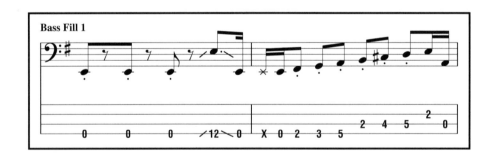
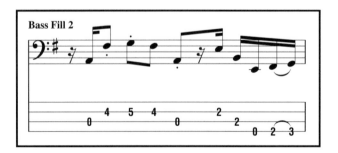

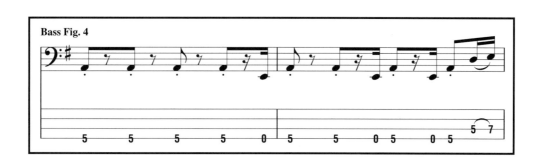

Heart and Soul

Words and Music by Mike Chapman and Nicky Chinn

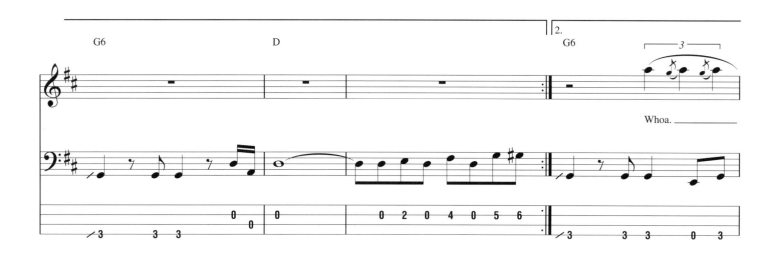
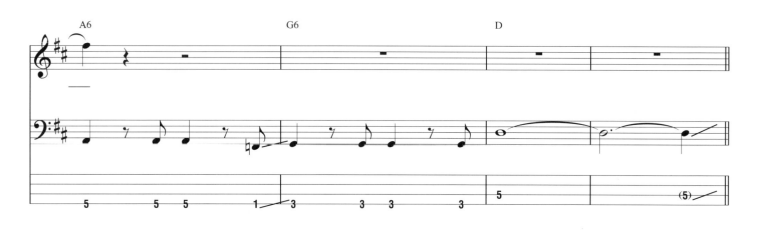
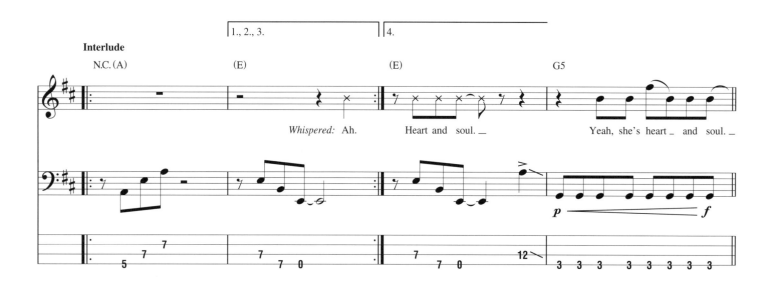
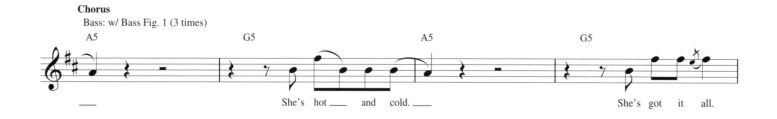

I Did It

Words and Music by David J. Matthews and Glen Ballard

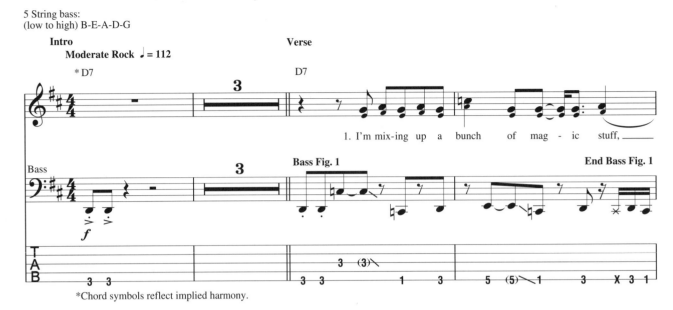

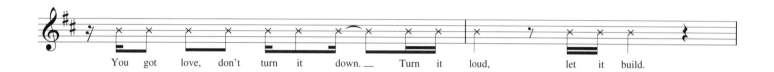
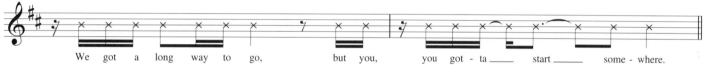

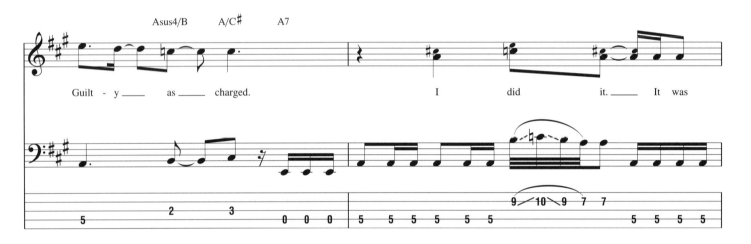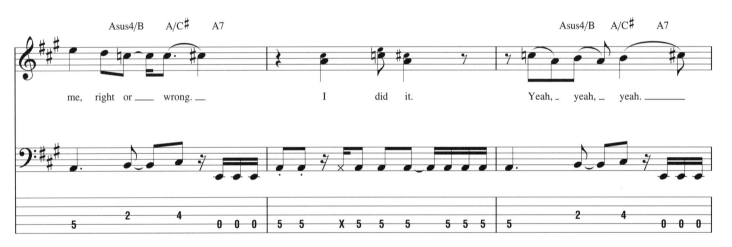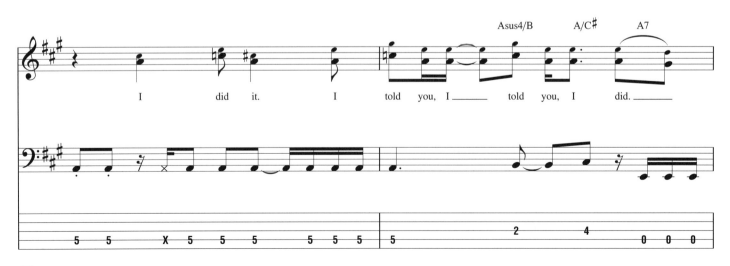

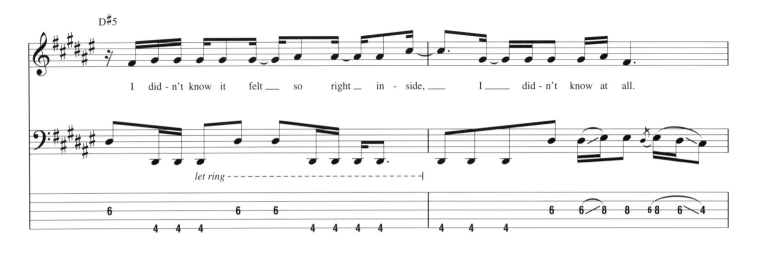
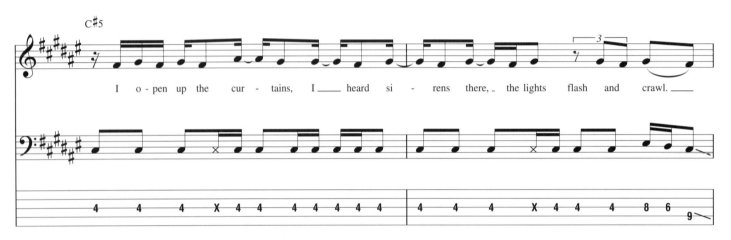

It Can Happen

Words and Music by John Anderson, Trevor Rabin and Chris Squire

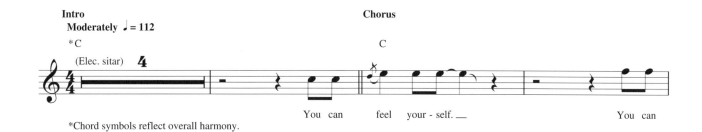
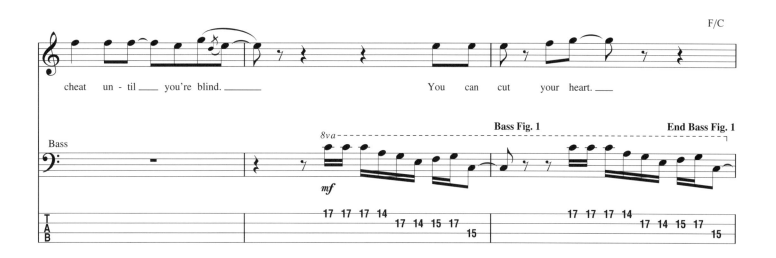

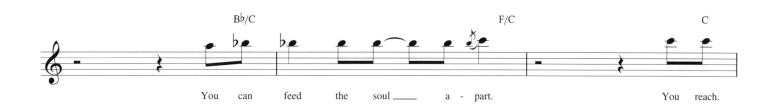
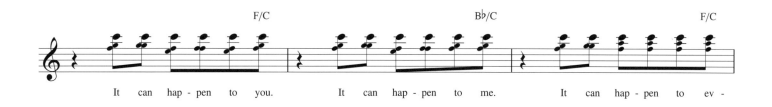

Copyright © 1983 by Carlin Music Corp., Tremander Songs, Affirmative Music and Warner-Tamerlane Publishing Corp.
All Rights for Carlin Music Corp. in the U.S. and Canada Administered by Carbert Music Inc.
International Copyright Secured All Rights Reserved
Used by Permission

Interlude

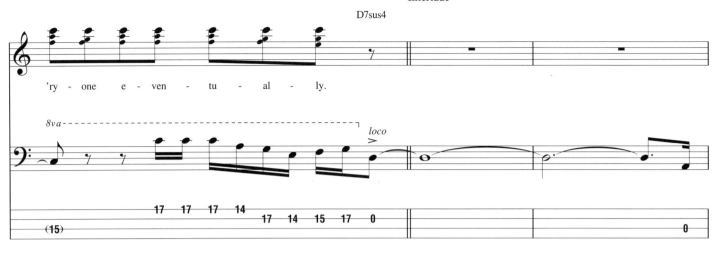

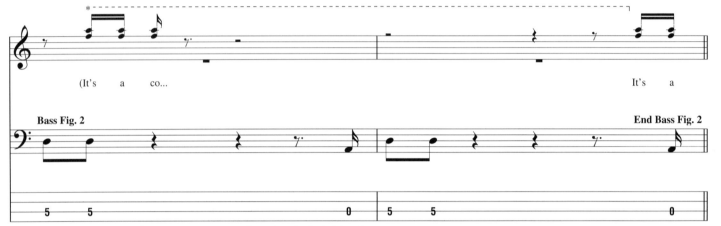

*w/ echo set for quarter-note regeneration and gradually fade in echo repeats.

Verse

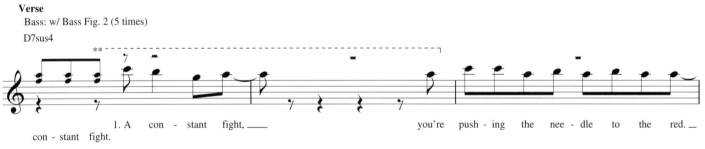

**Gradually fade out echo repeats.

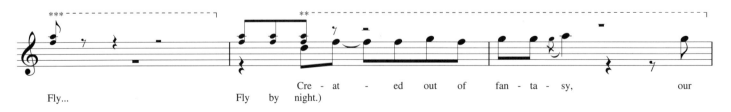

***Gradually fade in echo repeats.

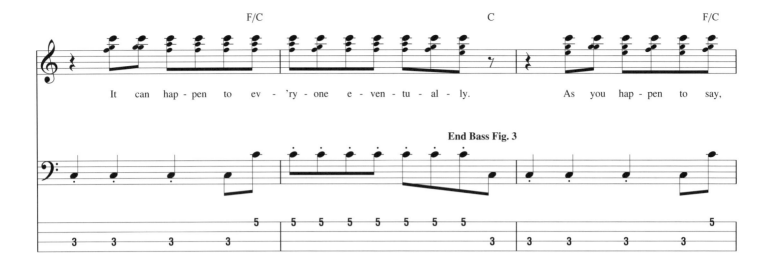
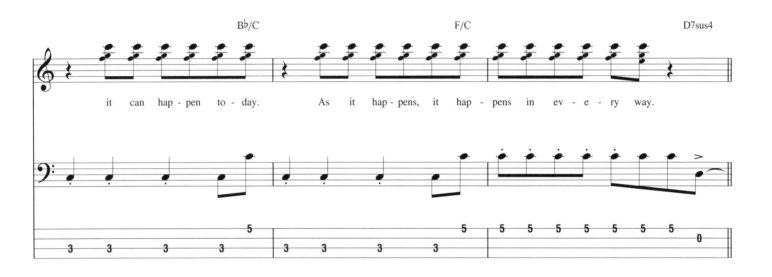

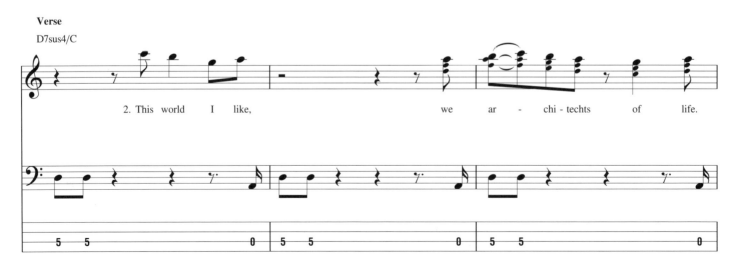

Chorus
Bass: w/ Bass Fig. 3 (2 1/2 times)

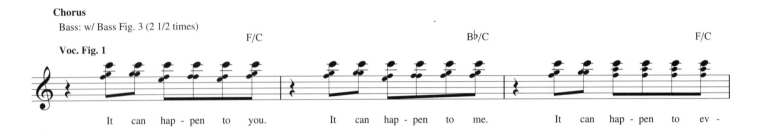

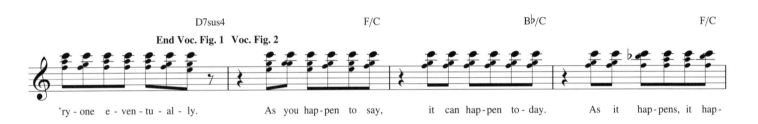

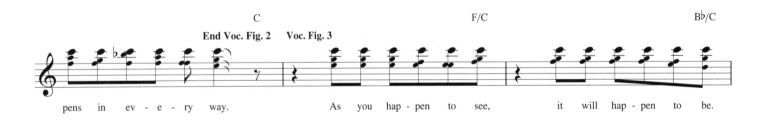

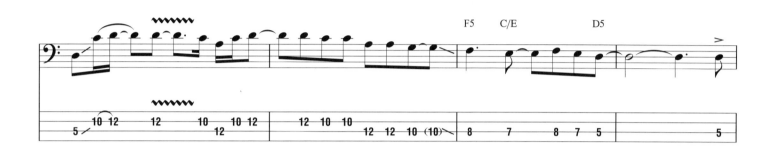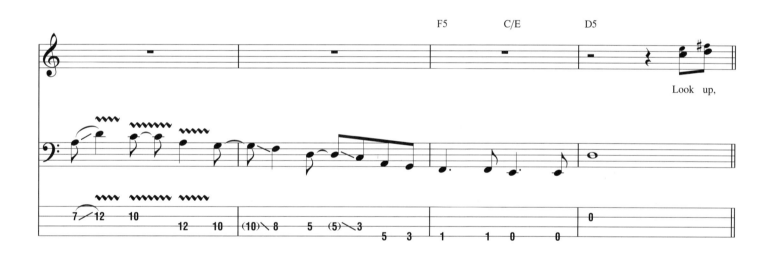

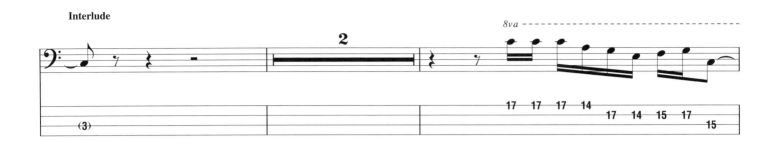
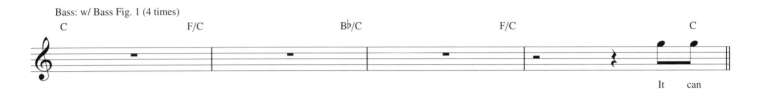
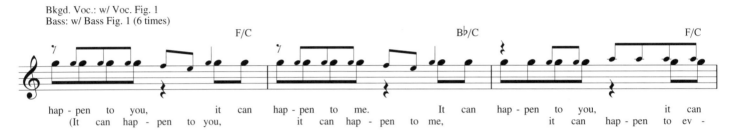

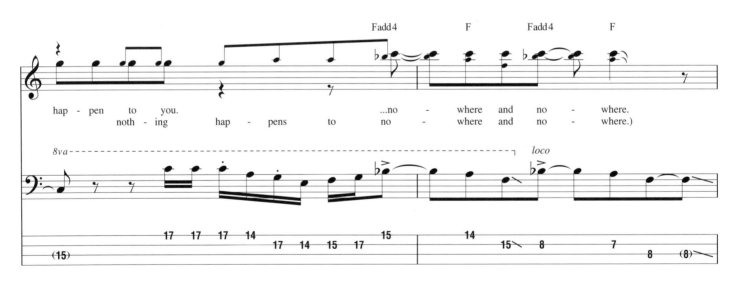

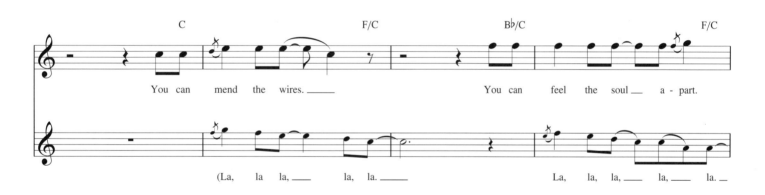

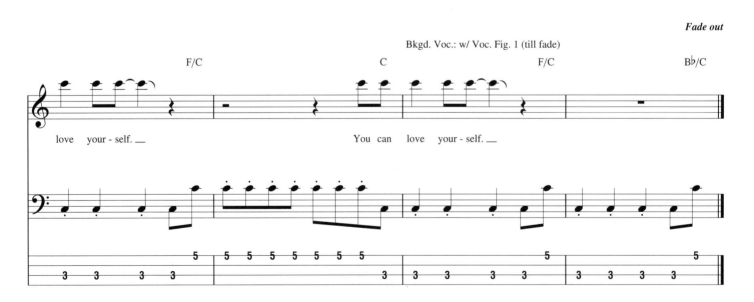

The Joker
Words and Music by Steve Miller, Eddie Curtis and Ahmet Ertegun

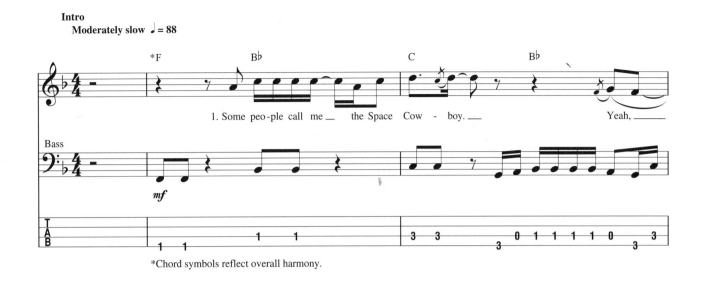

*Chord symbols reflect overall harmony.

Copyright © 1973 by Sailor Music and Warner-Tamerlane Publishing Corp.
Copyright Renewed
All Rights Reserved   Used by Permission

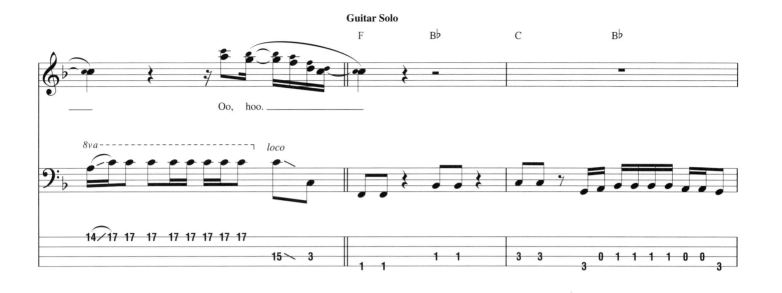
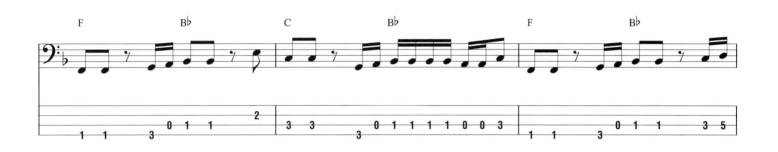

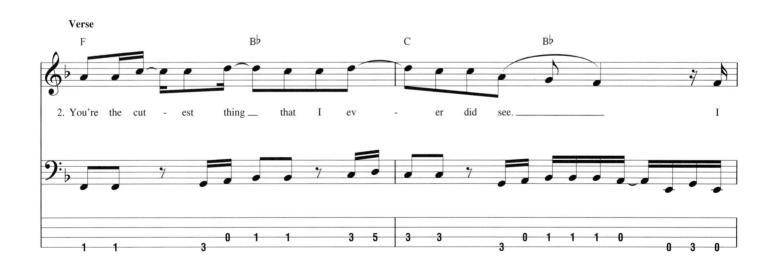

2. You're the cut - est thing _ that I ev - er did see. _ I

103

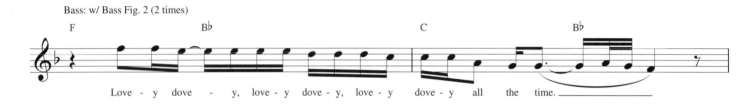
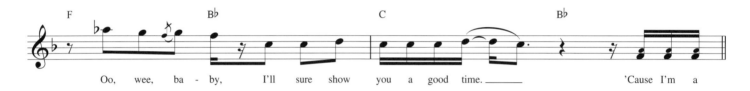

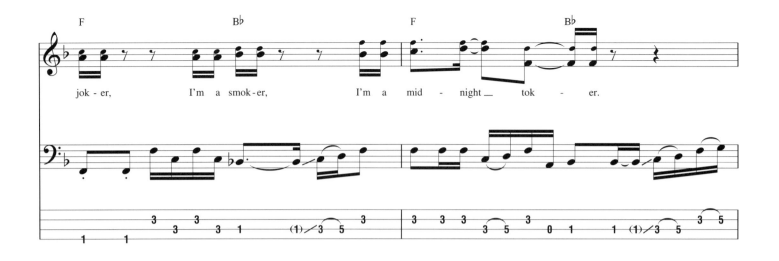

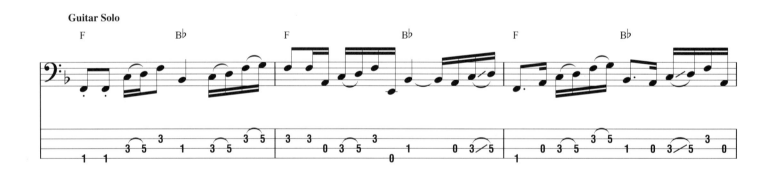
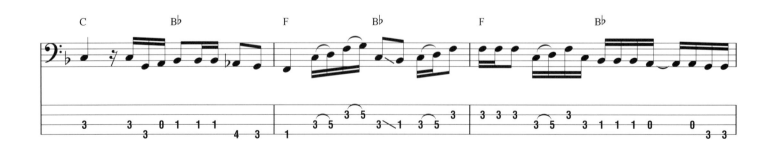

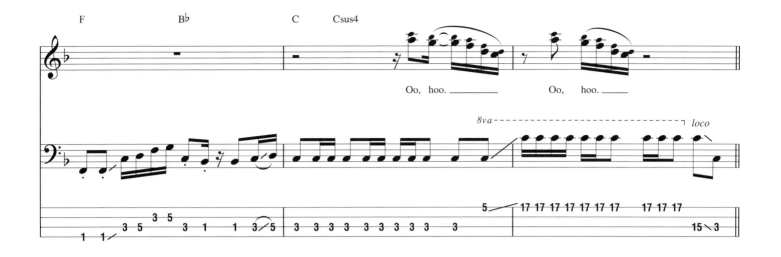

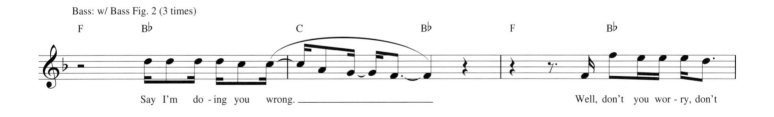

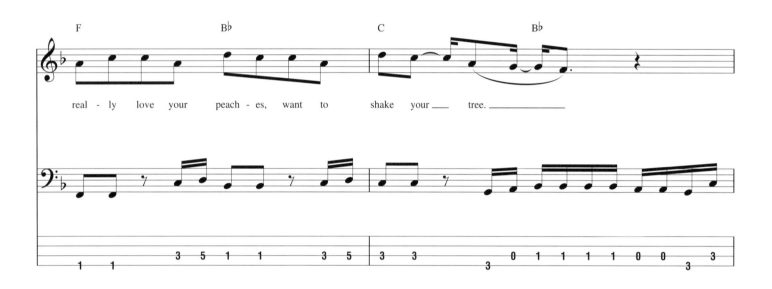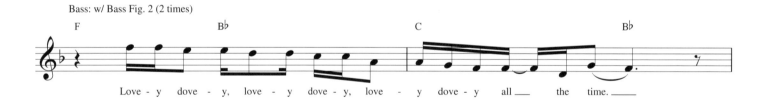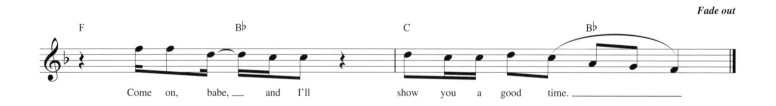

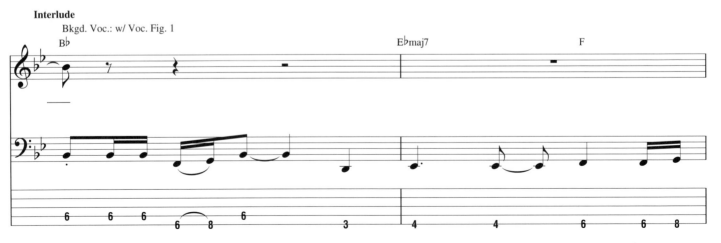

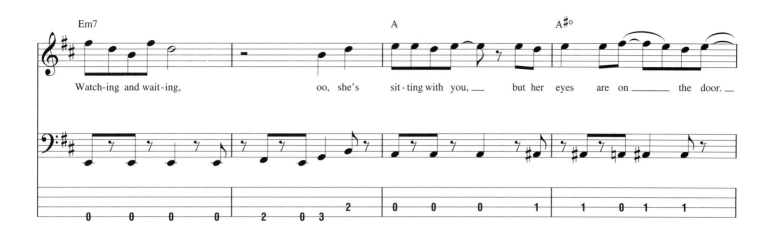

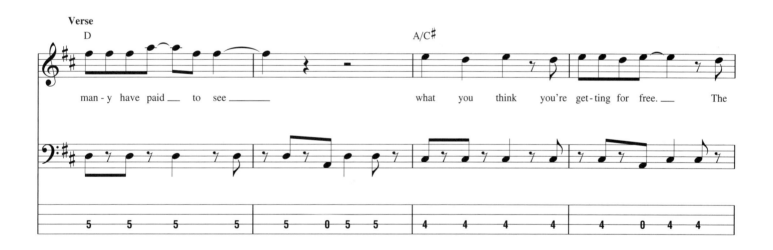
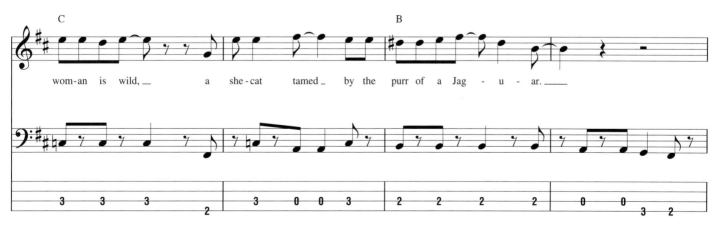

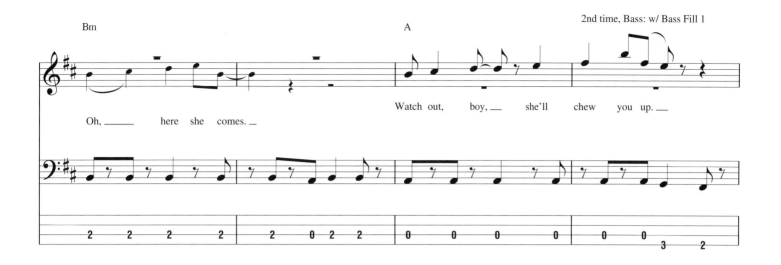

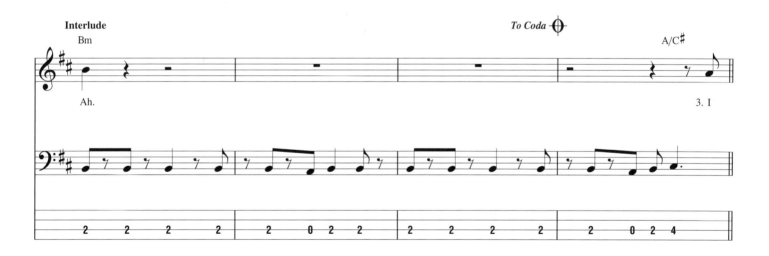
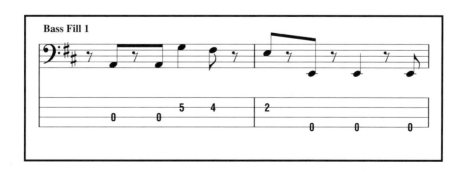

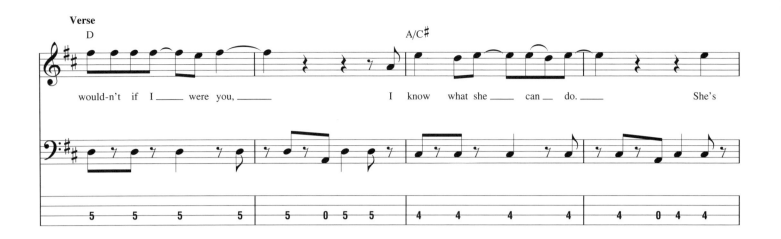
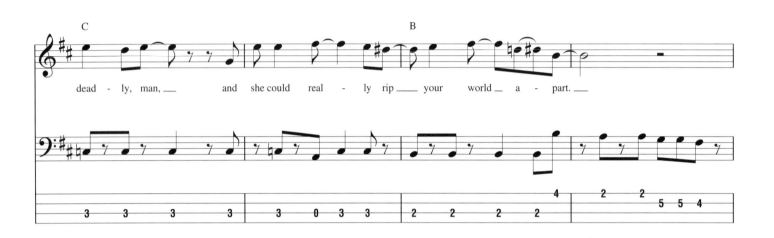
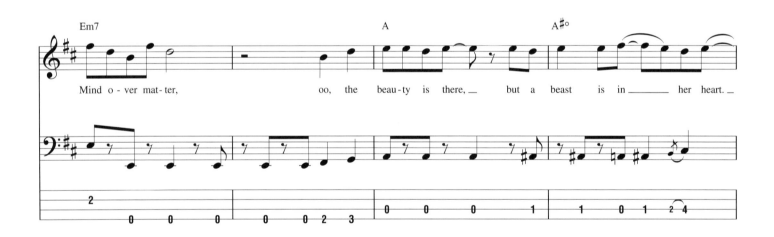
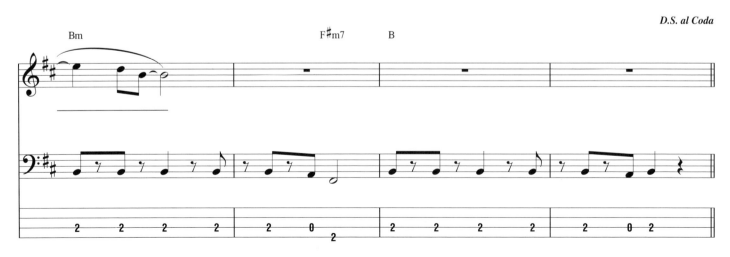

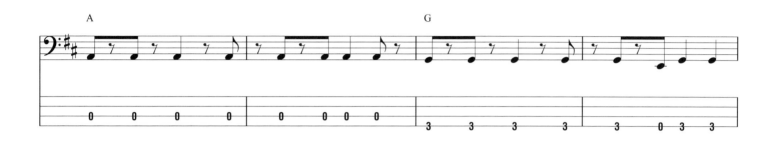

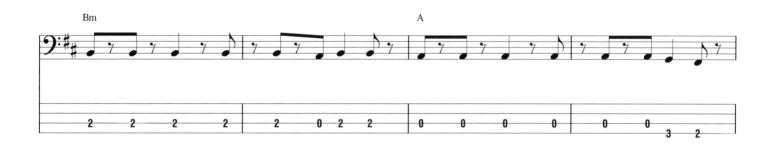
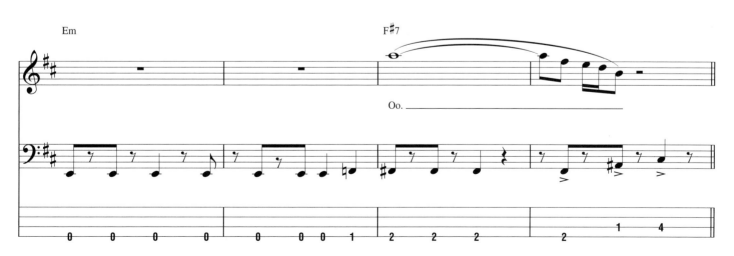

No Reply at All
Words and Music by Tony Banks, Phil Collins and Mike Rutherford

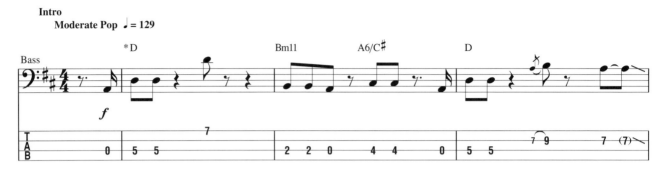

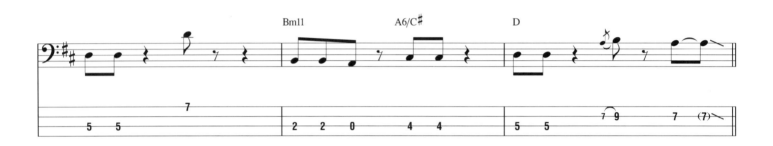

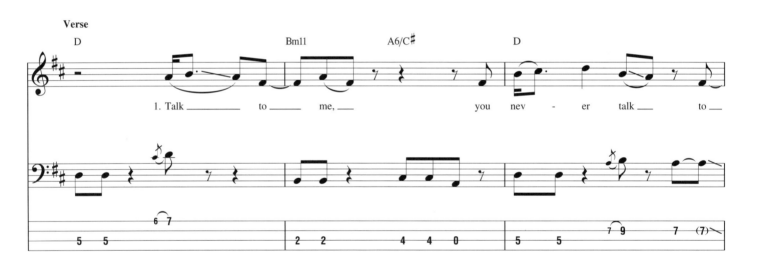

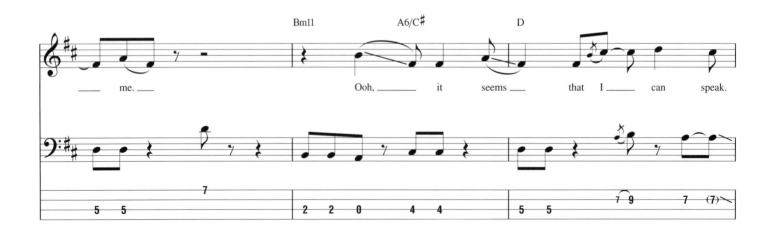

© 1981 ANTHONY BANKS LTD., PHILIP COLLINS LTD., MICHAEL RUTHERFORD LTD. and HIT & RUN MUSIC (PUBLISHING) LTD.
All Rights Controlled and Administered by EMI APRIL MUSIC INC.
All Rights Reserved   International Copyright Secured   Used by Permission

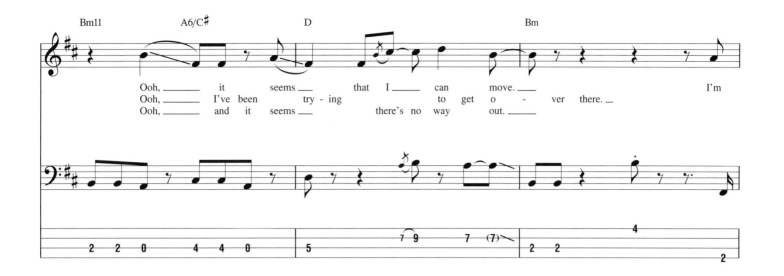
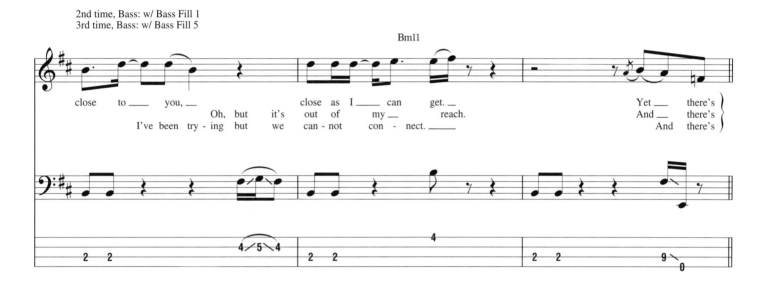
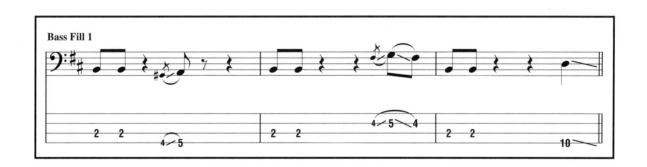
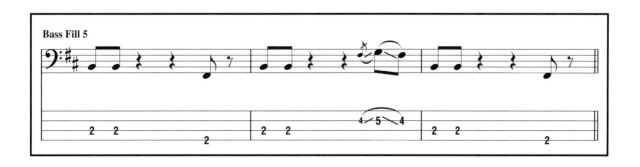

131

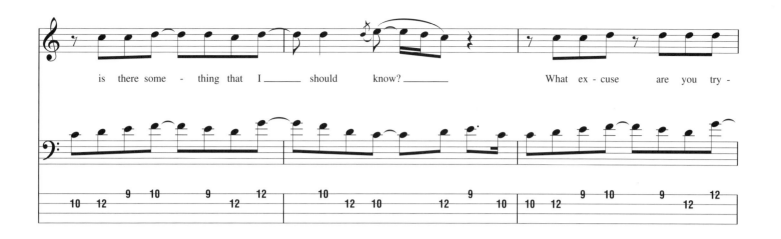
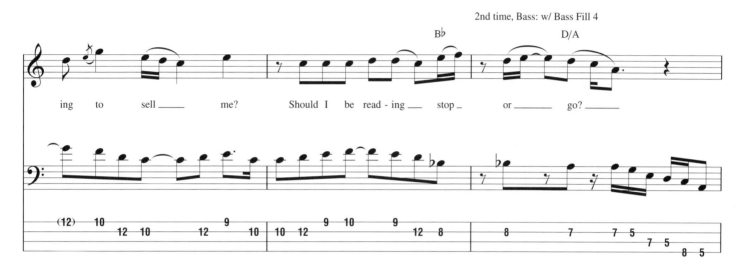

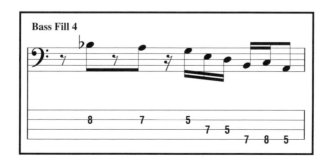

One Thing Leads to Another

Words and Music by Cy Curnin, Jamie West-Oram, Adam Woods, Rupert Greenall and Alfred Agius

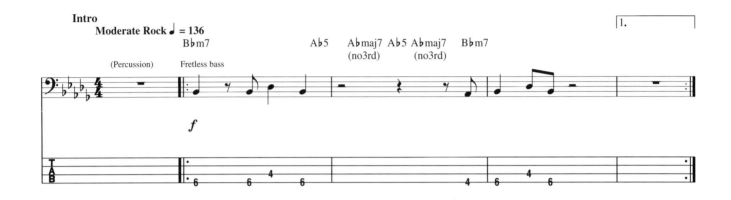

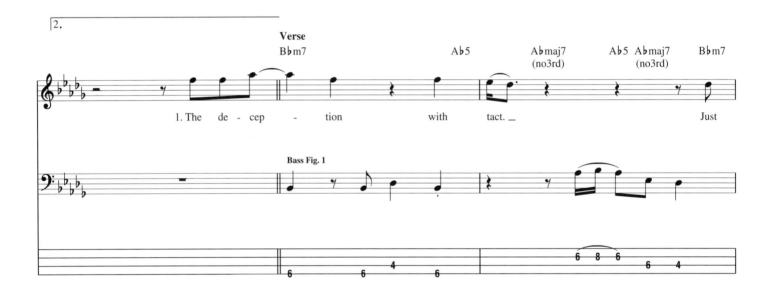

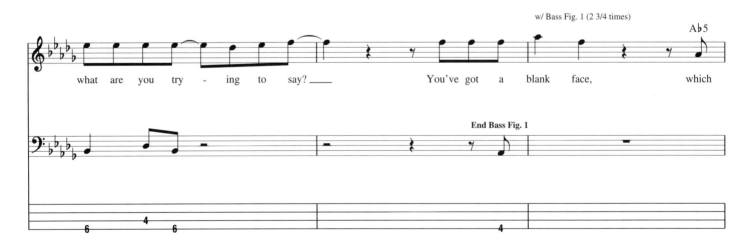

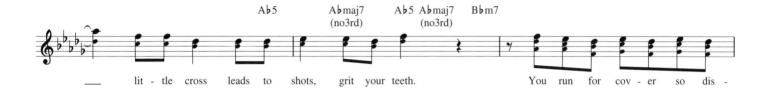

Chorus

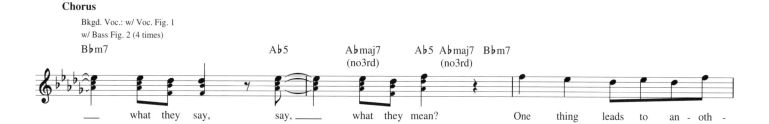
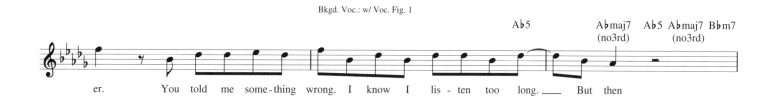

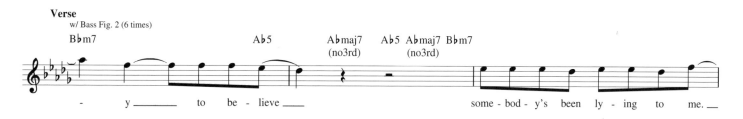

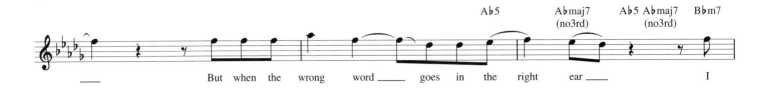

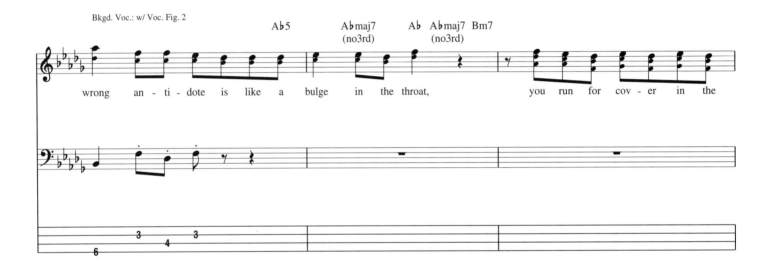
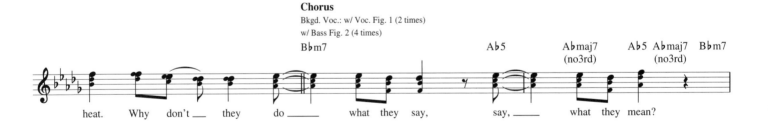

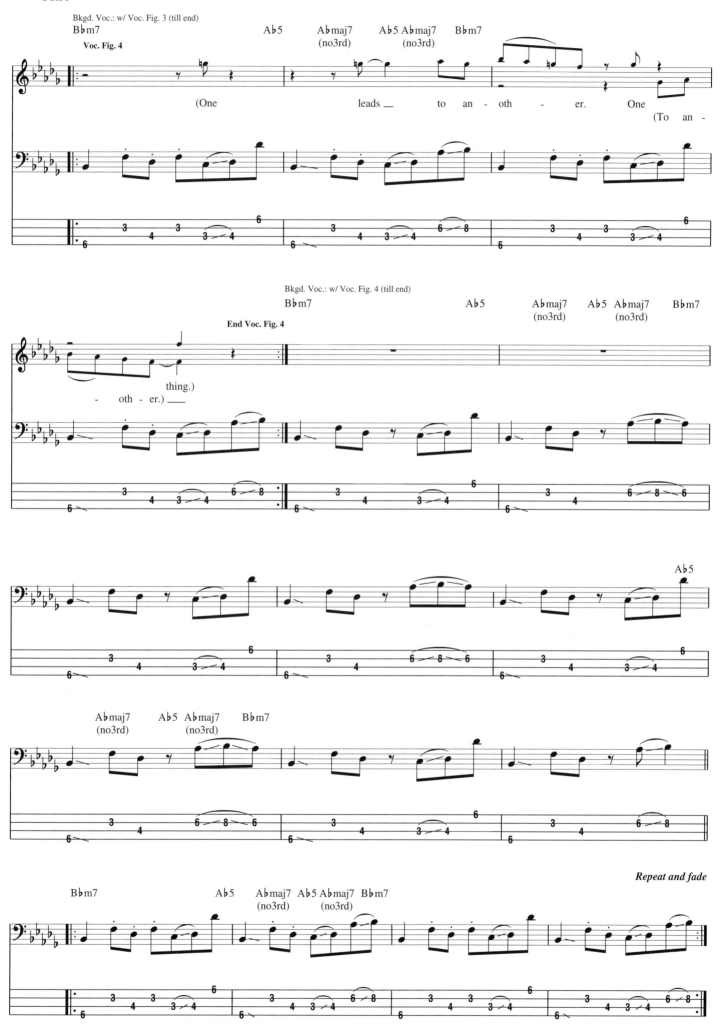

Rikki Don't Lose That Number

Words and Music by Walter Becker and Donald Fagen

Copyright © 1974 UNIVERSAL MUSIC CORP.
Copyright Renewed
All Rights Reserved   Used by Permission

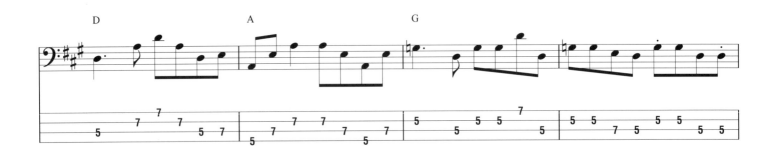
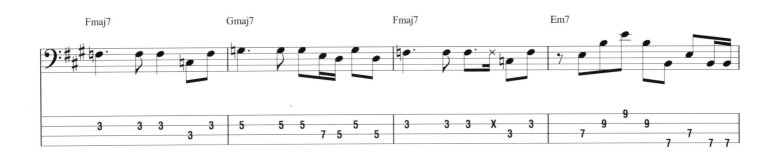
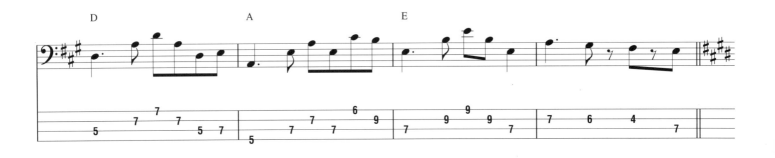

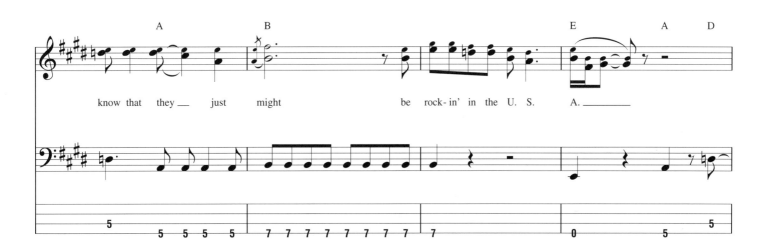
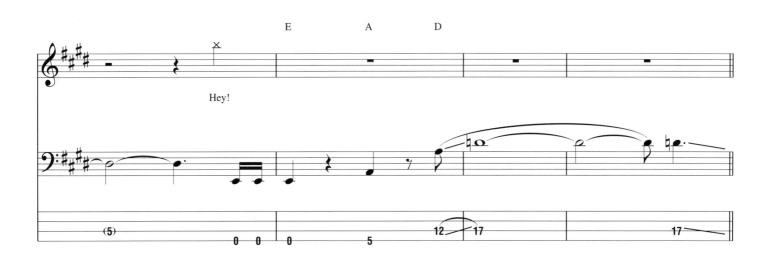

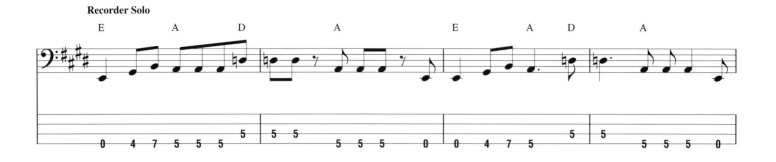
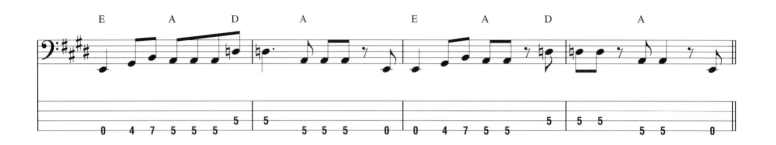

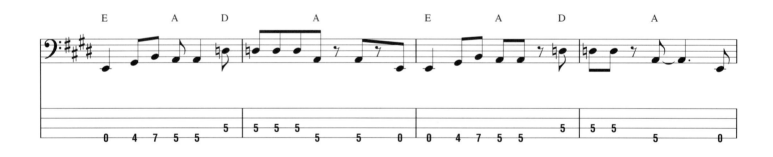
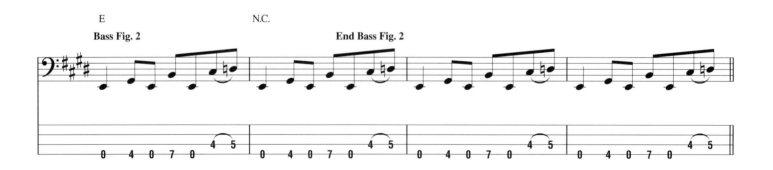

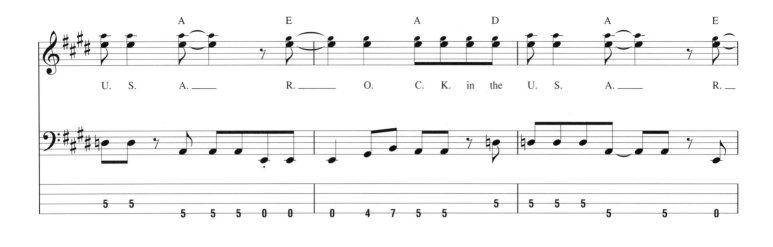
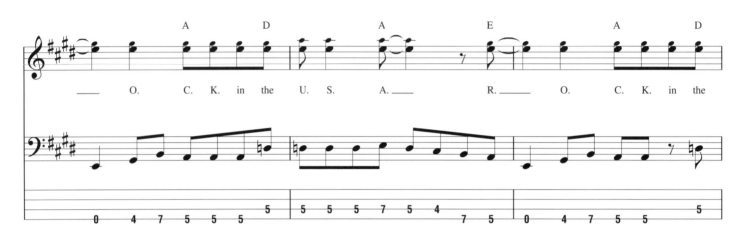
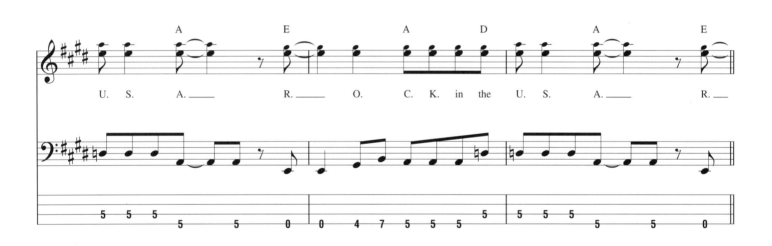

Smooth Operator

Words and Music by Helen Adu and Ray St. John

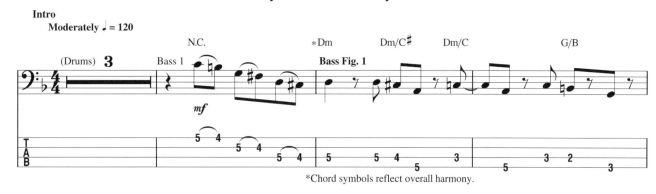

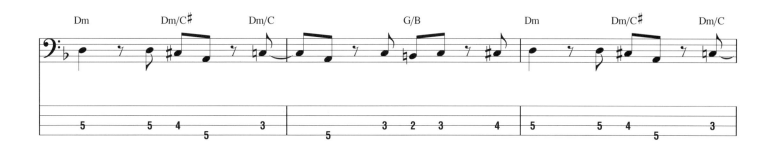

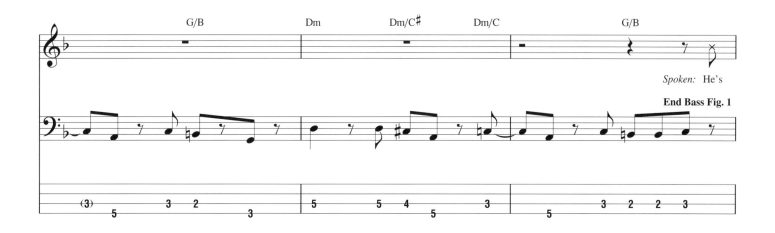

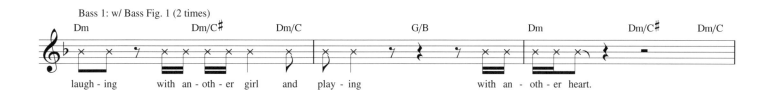

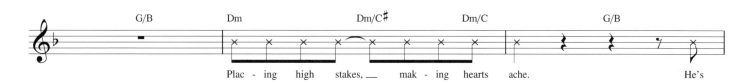

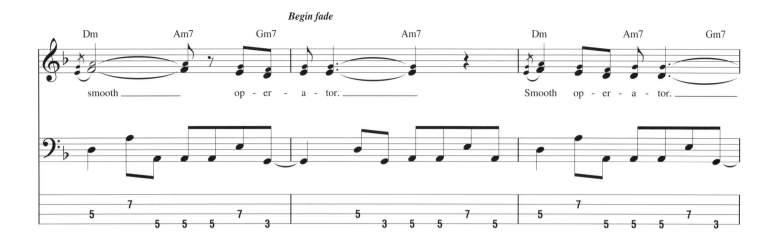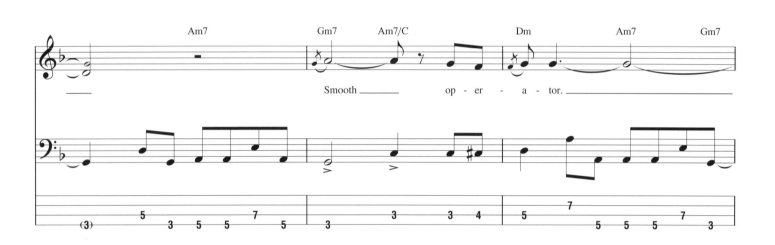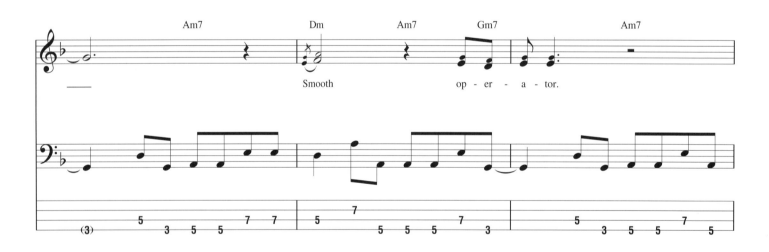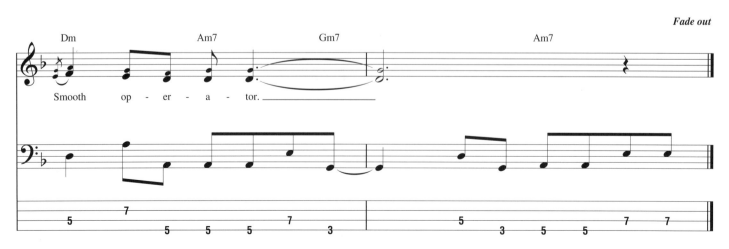

Stuck in the Middle with You

Words and Music by Gerry Rafferty and Joe Egan

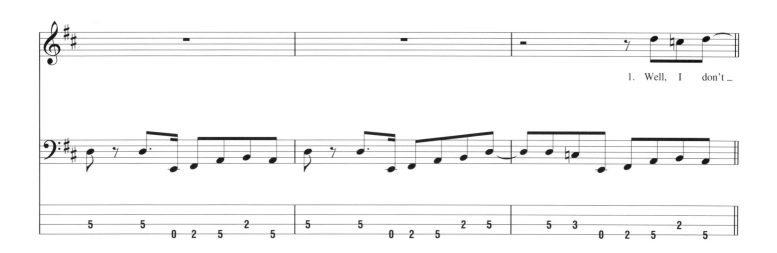

Copyright © 1973 UNIVERSAL - SONGS OF POLYGRAM INTERNATIONAL, INC. and BABY BUN MUSIC LTD.
Copyright Renewed
All Rights Reserved   Used by Permission

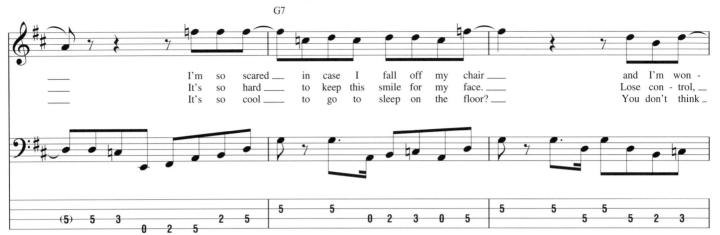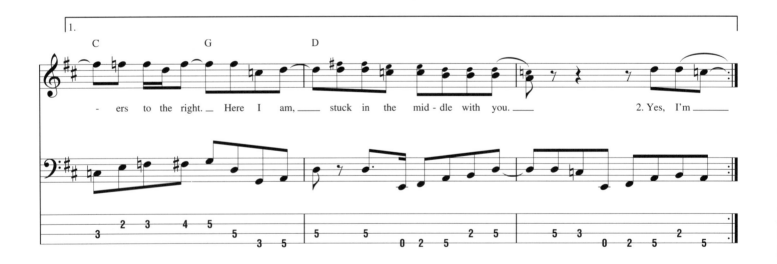

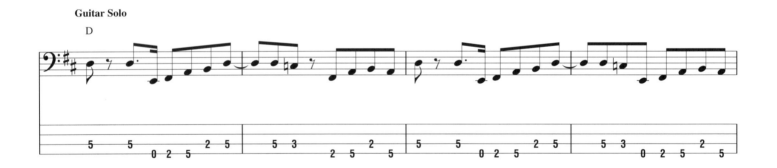

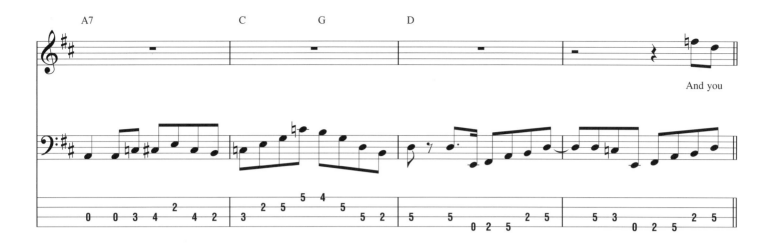

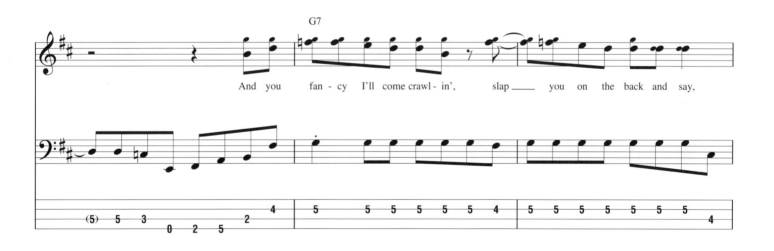
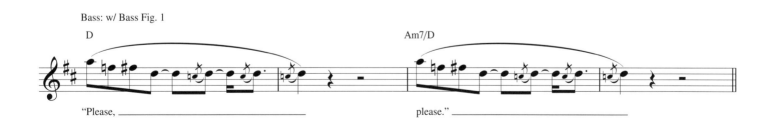

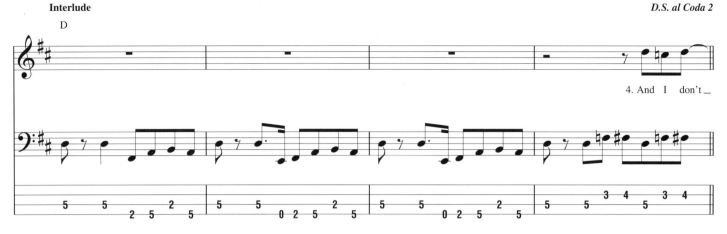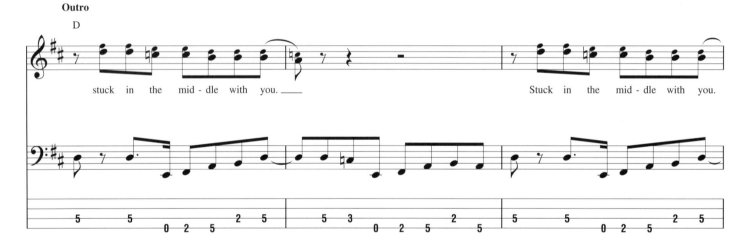

Suffragette City

Words and Music by David Bowie

© 1972 (Renewed 2000) EMI MUSIC PUBLISHING LTD., TINTORETTO MUSIC and MOTH MUSIC
All Rights for EMI MUSIC PUBLISHING LTD. Controlled and Administered by SCREEN GEMS-EMI MUSIC INC.
All Rights for TINTORETTO MUSIC Administered by RZO MUSIC
All Rights for MOTH MUSIC Administered by CHRYSALIS SONGS
All Rights Reserved International Copyright Secured Used by Permission

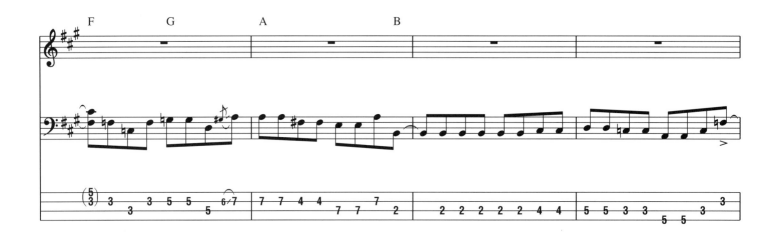

Thriller

Words and Music by Rod Temperton

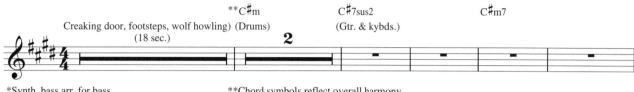

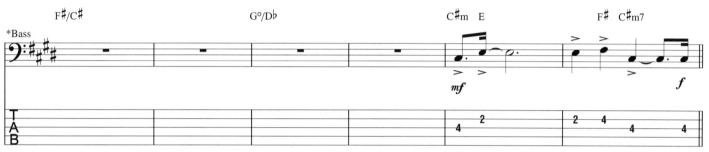

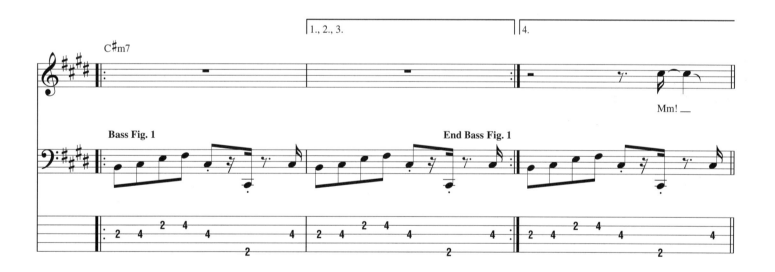

 Verse

1st time, Bass: w/ Bass Fig. 1 (8 times)
2nd time, Bass: w/ Bass Fig. 1 (7 1/2 times)
3rd time, Bass: w/ Bass Fig. 1 (3 1/2 times)

1. It's close to mid - night and some-thing e - vil's lurk-ing in the dark.
2. You hear the door slam and re - al - ize there's no-where left to run.
3. They're out to get you, there's de-mons clos-ing in on ev - 'ry side.

Copyright © 1982 RODSONGS
All Rights Administered by ALMO MUSIC CORP.
All Rights Reserved Used by Permission

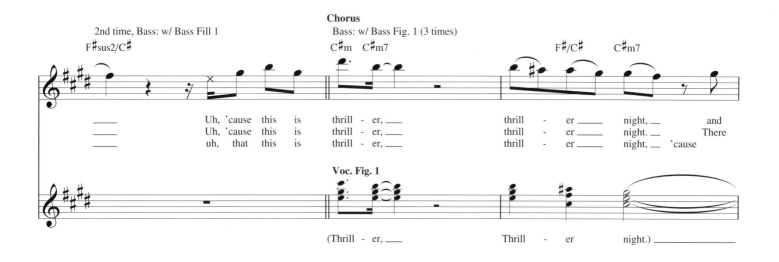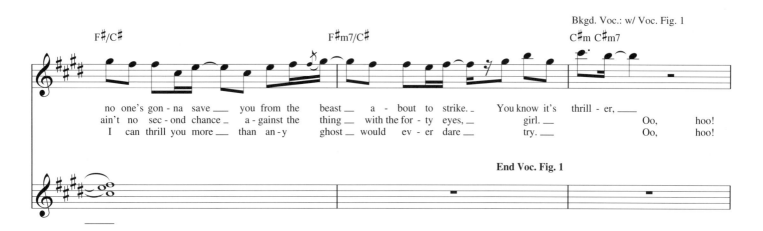

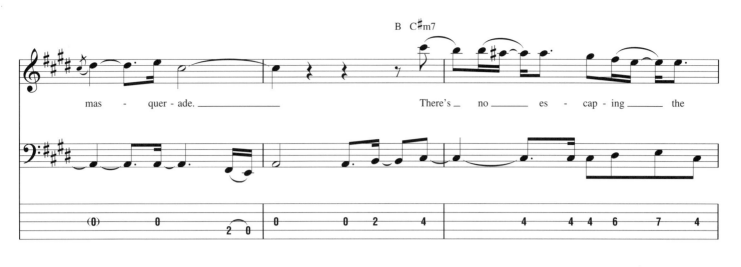

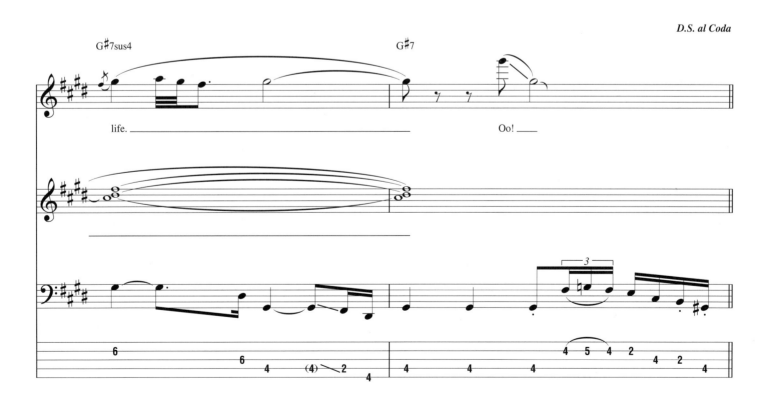

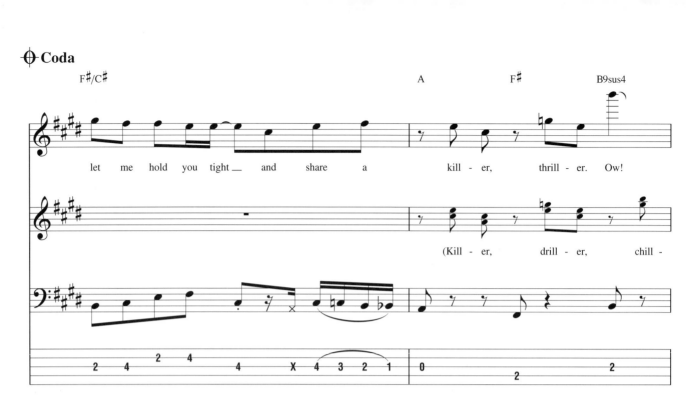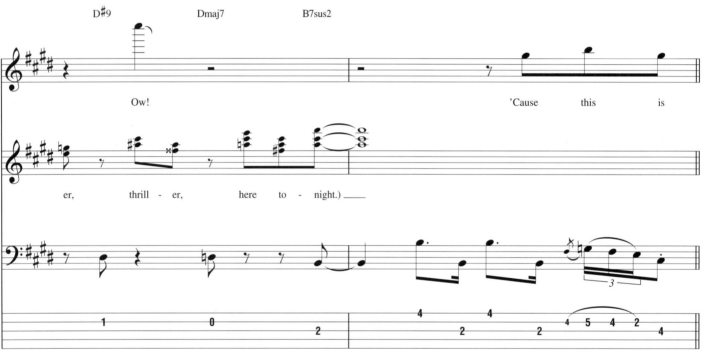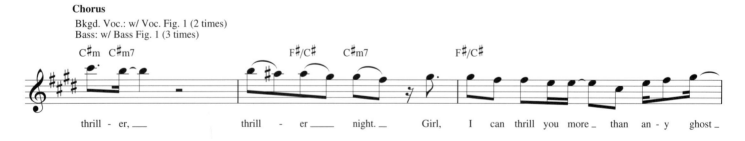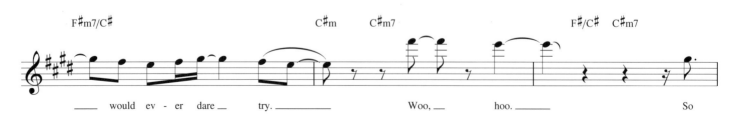

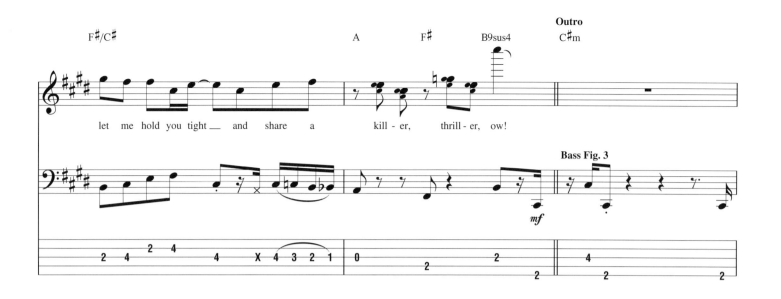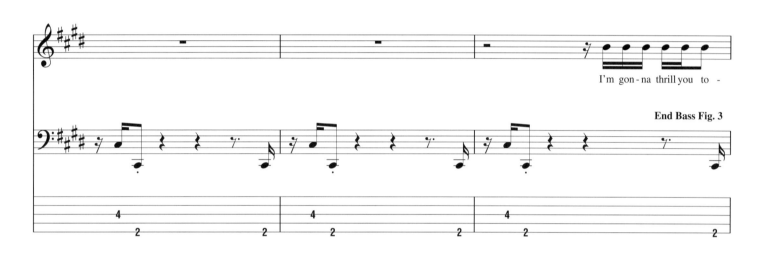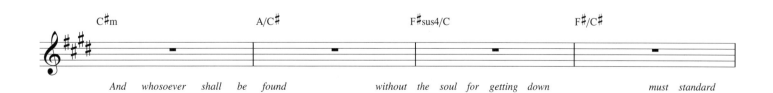

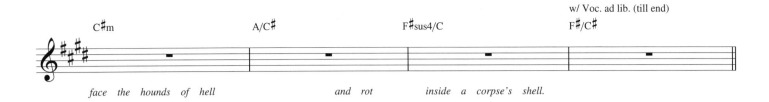
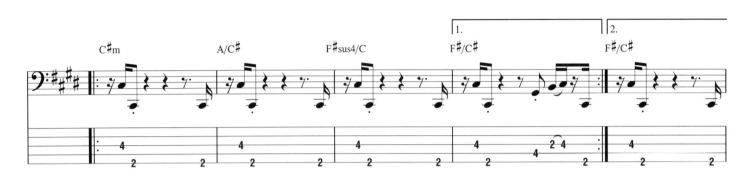
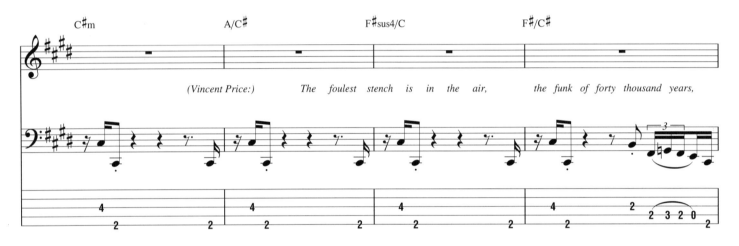
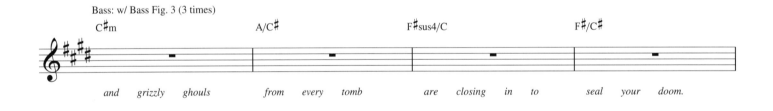
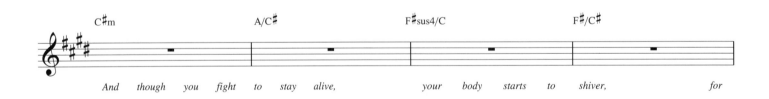
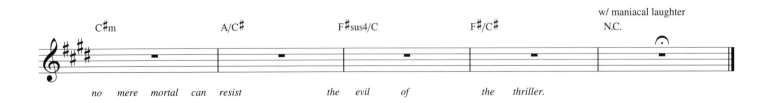

Turn the Page

Words and Music by Bob Seger

Copyright © 1973 Gear Publishing Co.
Copyright Renewed 2001
All Rights Reserved   Used by Permission

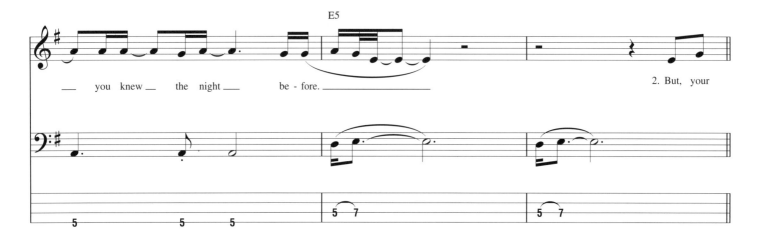

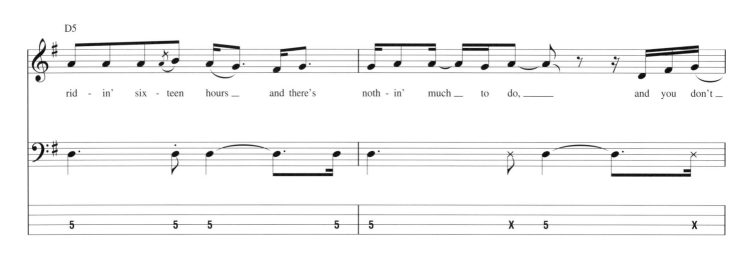

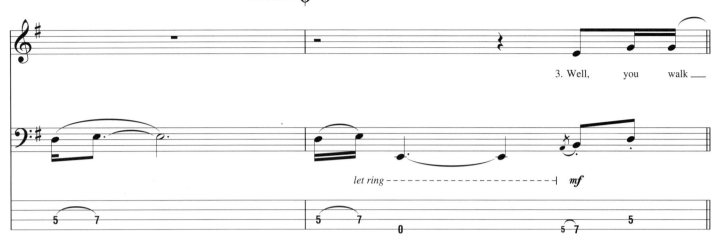
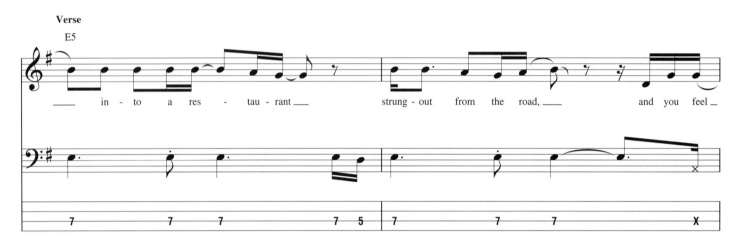
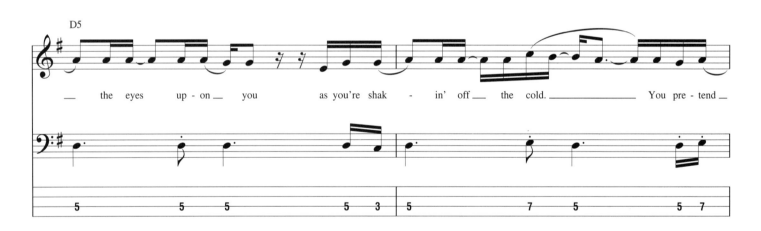
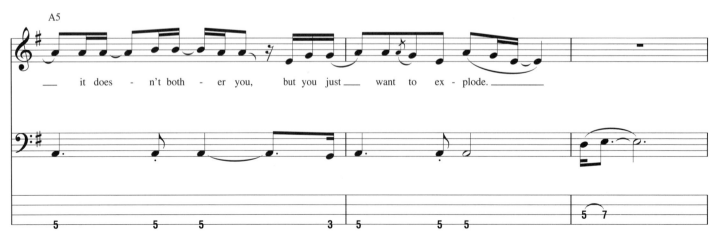

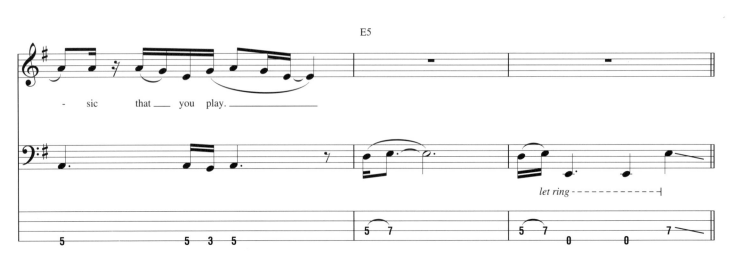
192

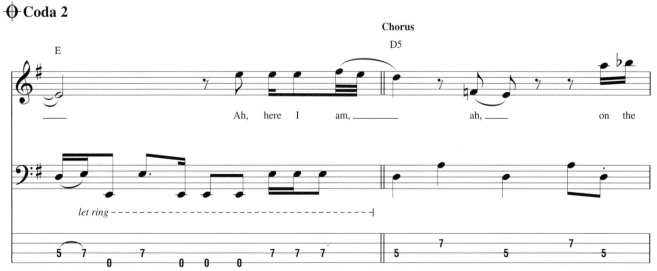

Werewolves of London

Words and Music by Warren Zevon, Robert Wachtel and LeRoy Marinel

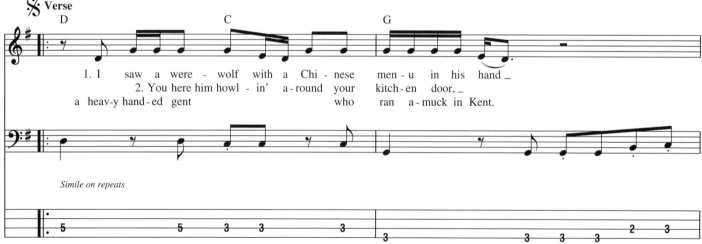

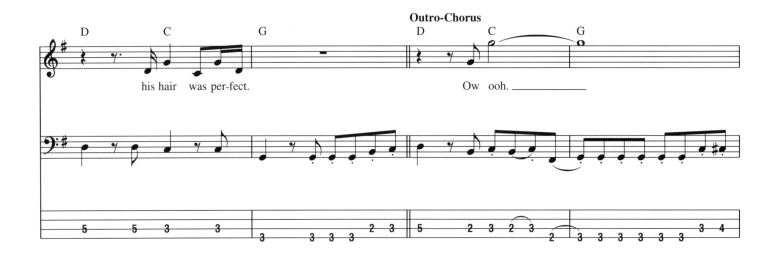

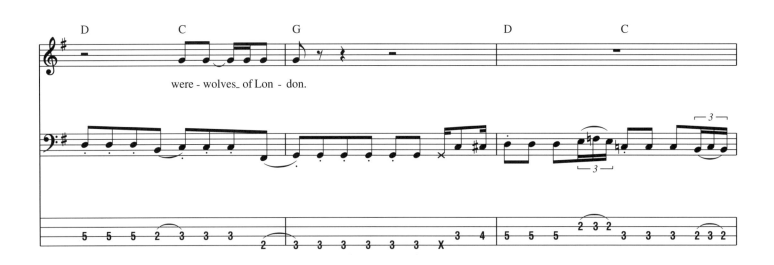

When the Heart Rules the Mind

Words and Music by Steven James Howe and Stephen Richard Hackett

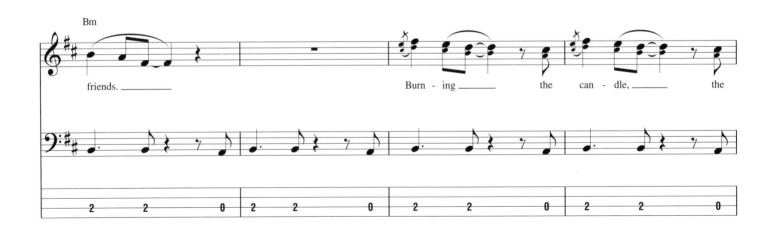

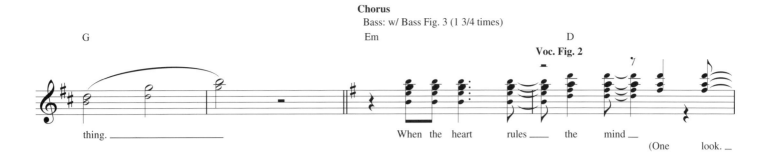
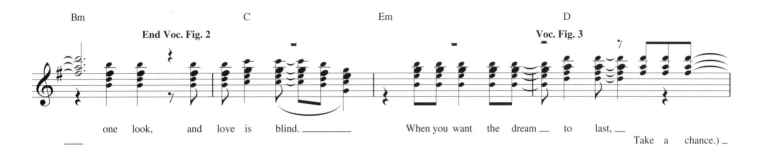
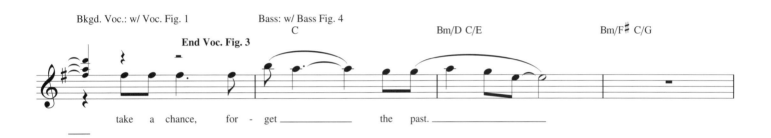
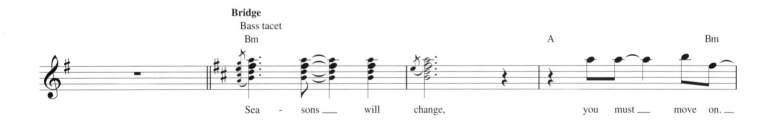

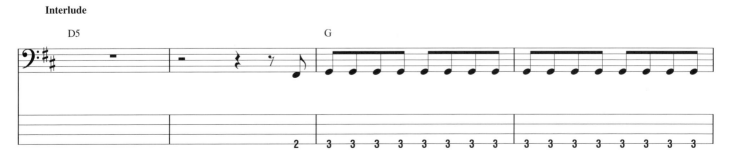

211

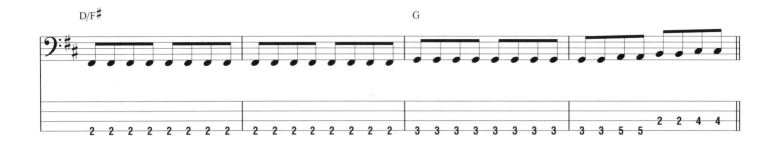

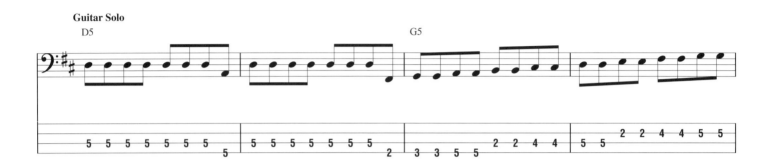

Guitar Solo

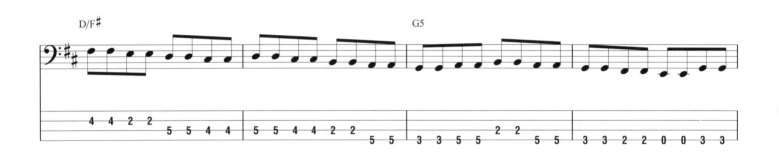

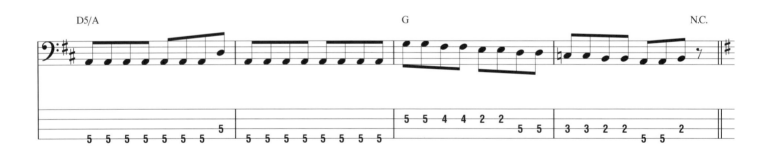

Interlude

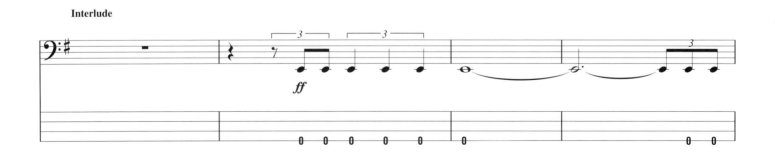

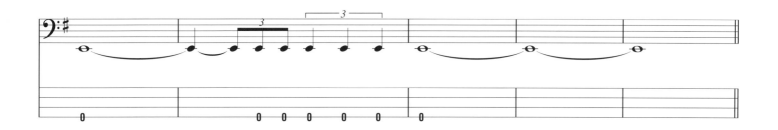

Chorus
Bass tacet

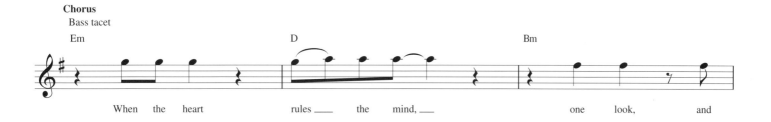

When the heart rules the mind, one look, and love is blind. When you want the dream to last,

take a chance, for-get the past. When the heart rules the mind

Bass: w/ Bass Fig. 3 (last 2 meas.)   Bass: w/ Bass Fig. 3 (4 3/4 times)

one look, and love is blind. When you want the dream to last

Voc. Fig. 4

(And love is blind. Take a chance.)

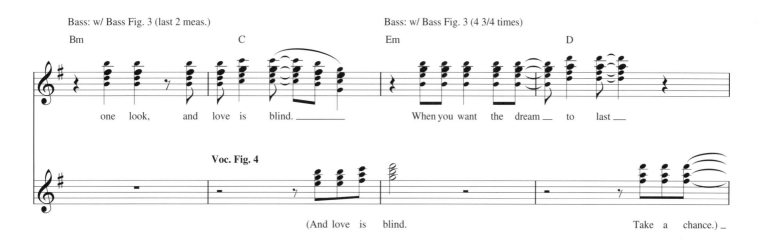

213

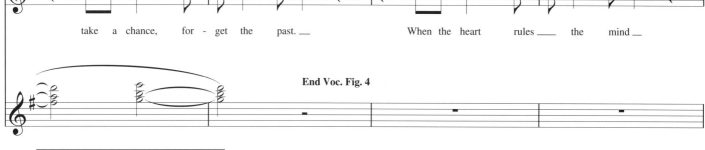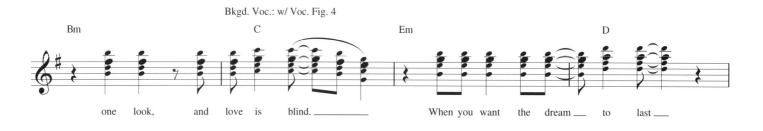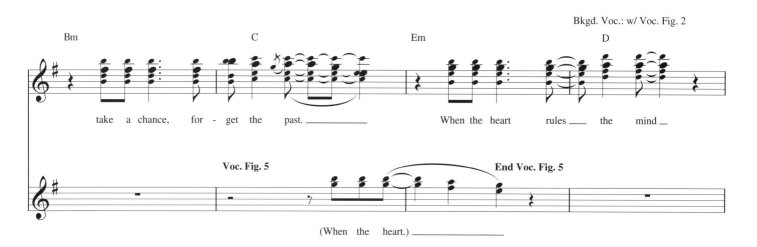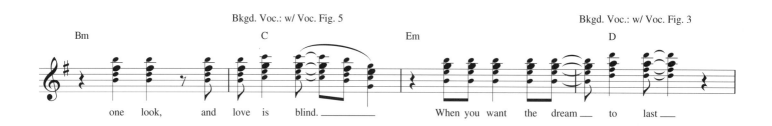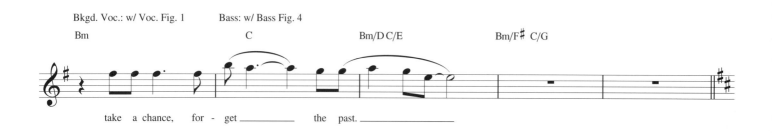

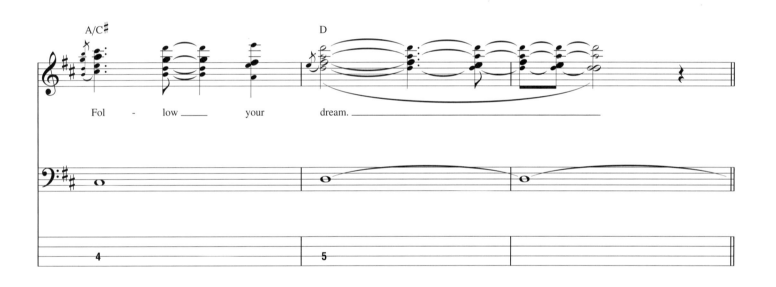
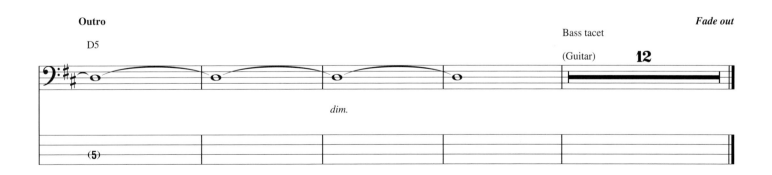

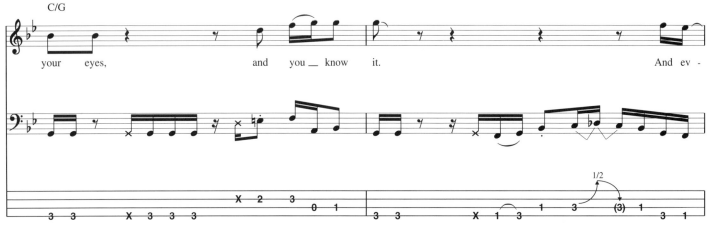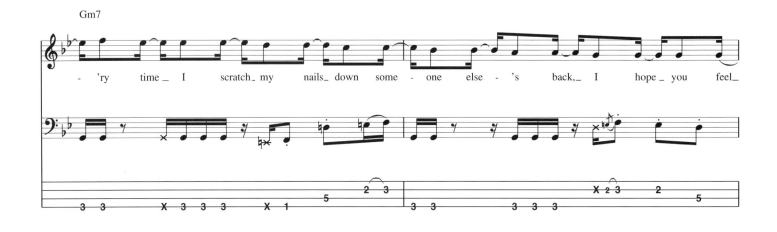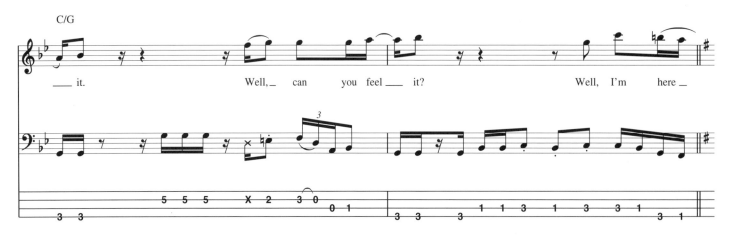

Bass Notation Legend

Bass music can be notated two different ways: on a *musical staff*, and in *tablature*.

THE MUSICAL STAFF shows pitches and rhythms and is divided by bar lines into measures. Pitches are named after the first seven letters of the alphabet.

TABLATURE graphically represents the bass fingerboard. Each horizontal line represents a string, and each number represents a fret.

HAMMER-ON: Strike the first (lower) note with one finger, then sound the higher note (on the same string) with another finger by fretting it without picking.

PULL-OFF: Place both fingers on the notes to be sounded. Strike the first note and without picking, pull the finger off to sound the second (lower) note.

LEGATO SLIDE: Strike the first note and then slide the same fret-hand finger up or down to the second note. The second note is not struck.

SHIFT SLIDE: Same as legato slide, except the second note is struck.

TRILL: Very rapidly alternate between the notes indicated by continuously hammering on and pulling off.

TREMOLO PICKING: The note is picked as rapidly and continuously as possible.

VIBRATO: The string is vibrated by rapidly bending and releasing the note with the fretting hand.

SHAKE: Using one finger, rapidly alternate between two notes on one string by sliding either a half-step above or below.

NATURAL HARMONIC: Strike the note while the fret hand lightly touches the string directly over the fret indicated.

MUFFLED STRINGS: A percussive sound is produced by laying the fret hand across the string(s) without depressing them and striking them with the pick hand.

BEND: Strike the note and bend up the interval shown.

BEND AND RELEASE: Strike the note and bend up as indicated, then release back to the original note. Only the first note is struck.

RIGHT-HAND TAP: Hammer ("tap") the fret indicated with the "pick-hand" index or middle finger and pull off to the note fretted by the fret hand.

LEFT-HAND TAP: Hammer ("tap") the fret indicated with the "fret-hand" index or middle finger.

SLAP: Strike ("slap") string with right-hand thumb.

POP: Snap ("pop") string with right-hand index or middle finger.

Additional Musical Definitions

 (accent) • Accentuate note (play it louder)

 (accent) • Accentuate note with great intensity

• (staccato) • Play the note short

⊓ • Downstroke

V • Upstroke

D.S. al Coda • Go back to the sign (𝄋), then play until the measure marked "**To Coda**," then skip to the section labelled "**Coda**."

D.C. al Fine • Go back to the beginning of the song and play until the measure marked "*Fine*" (end).

Bass Fig. • Label used to recall a recurring pattern.

Fill • Label used to identify a brief pattern which is to be inserted into the arrangement.

tacet • Instrument is silent (drops out).

• Repeat measures between signs.

 • When a repeated section has different endings, play the first ending only the first time and the second ending only the second time.

NOTE: Tablature numbers in parentheses mean:
1. The note is being sustained over a system (note in standard notation is tied), or
2. The note is sustained, but a new articulation (such as a hammer-on, pull-off, slide or vibrato begins), or
3. The note is a barely audible "ghost" note (note in standard notation is also in parentheses).